Public Health Advisor
Complete Self-Assessment Guide

D1784641

The guidance in this Self-Assessment is based on Public Health Advisor best practices and standards in business process architecture, design and quality management. The guidance is also based on the professional judgment of the individual collaborators listed in the Acknowledgments.

Notice of rights

You are licensed to use the Self-Assessment contents in your presentations and materials for internal use and customers without asking us - we are here to help.

Trademarks

Table of Contents

About The Art of Service

The Art of Service, Business Process Architects since 2000, is dedicated to helping stakeholders achieve excellence.

Defining, designing, creating, and implementing a process to solve a stakeholders challenge or meet an objective is the most valuable role… In EVERY group, company, organization and department.

Unless you're talking a one-time, single-use project, there should be a process. Whether that process is managed and implemented by humans, AI, or a combination of the two, it needs to be designed by someone with a complex enough perspective to ask the right questions.

Someone capable of asking the right questions and step back and say, 'What are we really trying to accomplish here? And is there a different way to look at it?'

With The Art of Service's Standard Requirements Self-Assessments, we empower people who can do just that — whether their title is marketer, entrepreneur, manager, salesperson, consultant, Business Process Manager, executive assistant, IT Manager, CIO etc... —they are the people who rule the future. They are people who watch the process as it happens, and ask the right questions to make the process work better.

Contact us when you need any support with this Self-Assessment and any help with templates, blue-prints and examples of standard documents you might need:

http://theartofservice.com
service@theartofservice.com

Acknowledgments

This checklist was developed under the auspices of The Art of Service, chaired by Gerardus Blokdyk.

Representatives from several client companies participated in the preparation of this Self-Assessment.

In addition, we are thankful for the design and printing services provided.

Included Resources - how to access

Included with your purchase of the book is the Public Health Advisor Self-Assessment Spreadsheet Dashboard which contains all questions and Self-Assessment areas and auto-generates insights, graphs, and project RACI planning - all with examples to get you started right away.

How? Simply send an email to
access@theartofservice.com
with this books' title in the subject to get the Public Health Advisor Self Assessment Tool right away.

You will receive the following contents with New and Updated specific criteria:

- The latest quick edition of the book in PDF

- The latest complete edition of the book in PDF, which criteria correspond to the criteria in...

- The Self-Assessment Excel Dashboard, and...

- Example pre-filled Self-Assessment Excel Dashboard to get familiar with results generation

- In-depth specific Checklists covering the topic

- Project management checklists and templates to assist with implementation

INCLUDES LIFETIME SELF ASSESSMENT UPDATES

Every self assessment comes with Lifetime Updates and Lifetime Free Updated Books. Lifetime Updates is an industry-first feature which allows you to receive verified self assessment updates, ensuring you always have the most accurate information at your fingertips.

Get it now- you will be glad you did - do it now, before you forget.

Send an email to **access@theartofservice.com** with this books' title in the subject to get the Public Health Advisor Self Assessment Tool right away.

Your feedback is invaluable to us

If you recently bought this book, we would love to hear from you! You can do this by writing a review on amazon (or the online store where you purchased this book) about your last purchase! As part of our continual service improvement process, we love to hear real client experiences and feedback.

How does it work?
To post a review on Amazon, just log in to your account and click on the Create Your Own Review button (under Customer Reviews) of the relevant product page. You can find examples of product reviews in Amazon. If you purchased from another online store, simply follow their procedures.

What happens when I submit my review?
Once you have submitted your review, send us an email at review@theartofservice.com with the link to your review so we can properly thank you for your feedback.

Purpose of this Self-Assessment

This Self-Assessment has been developed to improve understanding of the requirements and elements of Public Health Advisor, based on best practices and standards in business process architecture, design and quality management.

It is designed to allow for a rapid Self-Assessment to determine how closely existing management practices and procedures correspond to the elements of the Self-Assessment.

The criteria of requirements and elements of Public Health Advisor have been rephrased in the format of a Self-Assessment questionnaire, with a seven-criterion scoring system, as explained in this document.

In this format, even with limited background knowledge of Public

Health Advisor, a manager can quickly review existing operations to determine how they measure up to the standards. This in turn can serve as the starting point of a 'gap analysis' to identify management tools or system elements that might usefully be implemented in the organization to help improve overall performance.

How to use the Self-Assessment

On the following pages are a series of questions to identify to what extent your Public Health Advisor initiative is complete in comparison to the requirements set in standards.

To facilitate answering the questions, there is a space in front of each question to enter a score on a scale of '1' to '5'.

1 Strongly Disagree

2 Disagree

3 Neutral

4 Agree

5 Strongly Agree

Read the question and rate it with the following in front of mind:

**'In my belief,
the answer to this question is clearly defined'.**

There are two ways in which you can choose to interpret this statement;
1. how aware are you that the answer to the question is clearly defined
2. for more in-depth analysis you can choose to gather

evidence and confirm the answer to the question. This obviously will take more time, most Self-Assessment users opt for the first way to interpret the question and dig deeper later on based on the outcome of the overall Self-Assessment.

A score of '1' would mean that the answer is not clear at all, where a '5' would mean the answer is crystal clear and defined. Leave emtpy when the question is not applicable or you don't want to answer it, you can skip it without affecting your score. Write your score in the space provided.

After you have responded to all the appropriate statements in each section, compute your average score for that section, using the formula provided, and round to the nearest tenth. Then transfer to the corresponding spoke in the Public Health Advisor Scorecard on the second next page of the Self-Assessment.

Your completed Public Health Advisor Scorecard will give you a clear presentation of which Public Health Advisor areas need attention.

Public Health Advisor
Scorecard Example

Example of how the finalized Scorecard can look like:

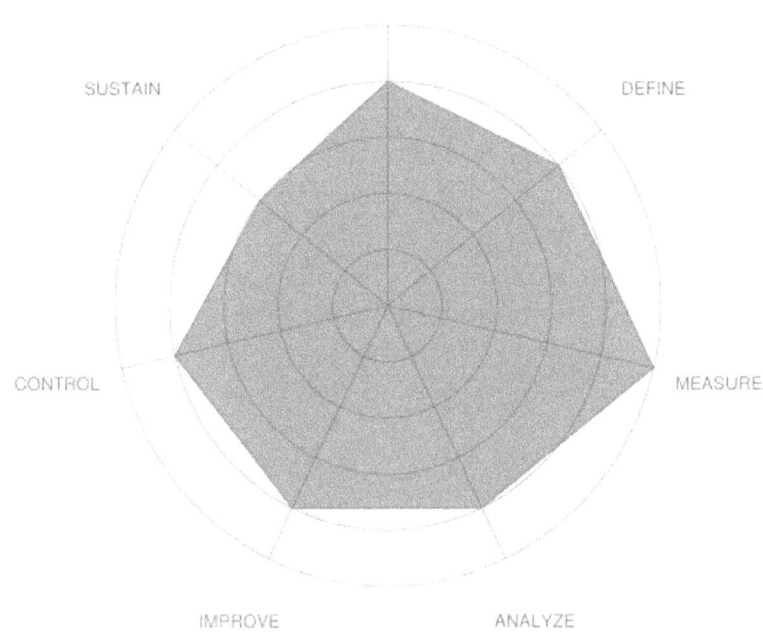

Public Health Advisor Scorecard

Your Scores:

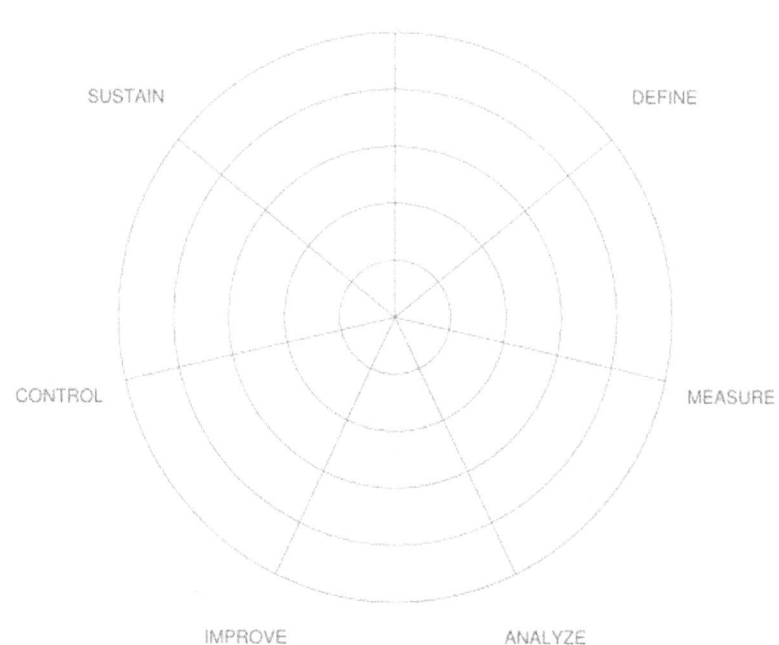

BEGINNING OF THE SELF-ASSESSMENT:

CRITERION #1: RECOGNIZE

INTENT: Be aware of the need for change. Recognize that there is an unfavorable variation, problem or symptom.

In my belief, the answer to this question is clearly defined:

5 Strongly Agree

4 Agree

3 Neutral

2 Disagree

1 Strongly Disagree

1. Who defines the rules in relation to any given issue?
<--- Score

2. What are the potential privacy issues?
<--- Score

3. What is the problem or issue?
<--- Score

4. What would happen if Public Health Advisor weren't done?
<--- Score

5. What information do users need?
<--- Score

6. What are the core problems that need to be addressed: for example, is it the number of providers, high turnover of staff or poor performance of available staff?
<--- Score

7. What extra resources will you need?
<--- Score

8. What is the role of public health in gang-membership prevention?
<--- Score

9. Act/Adjust: What Do you Need to Do Differently?
<--- Score

10. What does Public Health Advisor success mean to the stakeholders?
<--- Score

11. How does the changing health care environment inform what is needed in a new leader for your organization, including the ability to partner and knowledge of health care reform?
<--- Score

12. Who else hopes to benefit from it?
<--- Score

13. Do you need a privacy officer?

<--- Score

14. What is the smallest subset of the problem you can usefully solve?

<--- Score

15. Concerning public health issues that match the ccp?

<--- Score

16. What problems are you facing and how do you consider Public Health Advisor will circumvent those obstacles?

<--- Score

17. What assumptions need revision?

<--- Score

18. What projects do you need to kick off in order to execute this strategy?

<--- Score

19. Measuring the same people over time do you need to measure the same people over time, for example, to measure how perceived quality of health care increases or decreases?

<--- Score

20. How do you take a forward-looking perspective in identifying Public Health Advisor research related to market response and models?

<--- Score

21. How can auditing be a preventative security measure?

<--- Score

22. Is an authorization needed to share information with public health?
<--- Score

23. When a Public Health Advisor manager recognizes a problem, what options are available?
<--- Score

24. Should you invest in industry-recognized qualifications?
<--- Score

25. Are your goals realistic? Do you need to redefine your problem? Perhaps the problem has changed or maybe you have reached your goal and need to set a new one?
<--- Score

26. What is the big public health problem you aim to address with your program?
<--- Score

27. Is privacy a problem?
<--- Score

28. How much are sponsors, customers, partners, stakeholders involved in Public Health Advisor?
In other words, what are the risks, if Public Health Advisor does not deliver successfully?
<--- Score

29. What are the timeframes required to resolve each of the issues/problems?
<--- Score

30. What situation(s) led to this Public Health Advisor Self Assessment?
<--- Score

31. For your Public Health Advisor project, identify and describe the business environment, is there more than one layer to the business environment?
<--- Score

32. How are the Public Health Advisor's objectives aligned to the group's overall stakeholder strategy?
<--- Score

33. Are employees recognized or rewarded for performance that demonstrates the highest levels of integrity?
<--- Score

34. What are the expected benefits of Public Health Advisor to the stakeholder?
<--- Score

35. When do you need to have an authorization?
<--- Score

36. Will a response program recognize when a crisis occurs and provide some level of response?
<--- Score

37. What are the stakeholder objectives to be achieved with Public Health Advisor?
<--- Score

38. Are controls defined to recognize and contain problems?

<--- Score

39. Are there any specific expectations or concerns about the Public Health Advisor team, Public Health Advisor itself?
<--- Score

40. As a sponsor, customer or management, how important is it to meet goals, objectives?
<--- Score

41. Who needs to know about Public Health Advisor?
<--- Score

42. How are you going to measure success?
<--- Score

43. Have you identified your Public Health Advisor key performance indicators?
<--- Score

44. Think about the people you identified for your Public Health Advisor project and the project responsibilities you would assign to them. what kind of training do you think they would need to perform these responsibilities effectively?
<--- Score

45. Can family history be used as a tool for public health and preventive medicine?
<--- Score

46. Look at other systems - what do you need to tap into?
<--- Score

47. What are the significant effects of increased public health problems?

<--- Score

48. How does it fit into your organizational needs and tasks?

<--- Score

49. What does the public need from public health in your state or community?

<--- Score

50. What do you need to start doing?

<--- Score

51. Consider your own Public Health Advisor project, what types of organizational problems do you think might be causing or affecting your problem, based on the work done so far?

<--- Score

52. Do you need to amend your privacy notices?

<--- Score

53. How do program recipients think the public health issue should be addressed?

<--- Score

54. What problems are likely to occur during implementation?

<--- Score

55. Are you addressing the real problem or issue?

<--- Score

56. What is the role of multinational corporations

in addressing public health issues?
<--- Score

57. How extensively have you engaged a variety of health care and social service providers to coordinate transitions of care and address underlying needs/concerns?
<--- Score

58. Does every website need a privacy policy?
<--- Score

59. To what extent does each concerned units management team recognize Public Health Advisor as an effective investment?
<--- Score

Add up total points for this section:
_ _ _ _ _ = Total points for this section

Divided by: _ _ _ _ _ _ (number of statements answered) = _ _ _ _ _ _
Average score for this section

Transfer your score to the Public Health Advisor Index at the beginning of the Self-Assessment.

CRITERION #2: DEFINE:

INTENT: Formulate the stakeholder problem. Define the problem, needs and objectives.

In my belief, the answer to this question is clearly defined:

5 Strongly Agree

4 Agree

3 Neutral

2 Disagree

1 Strongly Disagree

1. What is the definition of success?
<--- Score

2. Is there a completed, verified, and validated high-level 'as is' (not 'should be' or 'could be') stakeholder process map?
<--- Score

3. How will the Public Health Advisor team and the

group measure complete success of Public Health Advisor?

<--- Score

4. Is full participation by members in regularly held team meetings guaranteed?

<--- Score

5. Are different versions of process maps needed to account for the different types of inputs?

<--- Score

6. Does the team have regular meetings?

<--- Score

7. Is this a HIPAA requirement?

<--- Score

8. Has a team charter been developed and communicated?

<--- Score

9. Has the Public Health Advisor work been fairly and/ or equitably divided and delegated among team members who are qualified and capable to perform the work? Has everyone contributed?

<--- Score

10. Is there any additional Public Health Advisor definition of success?

<--- Score

11. Has the direction changed at all during the course of Public Health Advisor? If so, when did it change and why?

<--- Score

12. Is the team adequately staffed with the desired cross-functionality? If not, what additional resources are available to the team?
<--- Score

13. How is the team tracking and documenting its work?
<--- Score

14. Is special Public Health Advisor user knowledge required?
<--- Score

15. Is the team formed and are team leaders (Coaches and Management Leads) assigned?
<--- Score

16. How do you think the partners involved in Public Health Advisor would have defined success?
<--- Score

17. Is Public Health Advisor currently on schedule according to the plan?
<--- Score

18. Is Public Health Advisor linked to key stakeholder goals and objectives?
<--- Score

19. Is there regularly 100% attendance at the team meetings? If not, have appointed substitutes attended to preserve cross-functionality and full representation?
<--- Score

20. Have the customer needs been translated into specific, measurable requirements? How?
<--- Score

21. Is the team sponsored by a champion or stakeholder leader?
<--- Score

22. Has/have the customer(s) been identified?
<--- Score

23. If substitutes have been appointed, have they been briefed on the Public Health Advisor goals and received regular communications as to the progress to date?
<--- Score

24. How do you manage scope?
<--- Score

25. Do you have projects that require a HIPAA-Compliant authorization?
<--- Score

26. Has the improvement team collected the 'voice of the customer' (obtained feedback – qualitative and quantitative)?
<--- Score

27. Are team charters developed?
<--- Score

28. Has anyone else (internal or external to the group) attempted to solve this problem or a similar one before? If so, what knowledge can be leveraged from these previous efforts?

<--- Score

29. Do the problem and goal statements meet the SMART criteria (specific, measurable, attainable, relevant, and time-bound)?
<--- Score

30. Has everyone on the team, including the team leaders, been properly trained?
<--- Score

31. The political context: who holds power?
<--- Score

32. Do you all define Public Health Advisor in the same way?
<--- Score

33. Will team members regularly document their Public Health Advisor work?
<--- Score

34. What happens if Public Health Advisor's scope changes?
<--- Score

35. What are the rough order estimates on cost savings/opportunities that Public Health Advisor brings?
<--- Score

36. How do you keep key subject matter experts in the loop?
<--- Score

37. How did the Public Health Advisor manager

receive input to the development of a Public Health Advisor improvement plan and the estimated completion dates/times of each activity?
<--- Score

38. How was the 'as is' process map developed, reviewed, verified and validated?
<--- Score

39. Is there a critical path to deliver Public Health Advisor results?
<--- Score

40. Are there any constraints known that bear on the ability to perform Public Health Advisor work? How is the team addressing them?
<--- Score

41. Will beneficiaries that receive services from a health care professional or provider that is a part of an ACO be required to receive all his/her services from the ACO?
<--- Score

42. What are the tasks and definitions?
<--- Score

43. What is the definition of Public Health Advisor excellence?
<--- Score

44. What are the boundaries of the scope? What is in bounds and what is not? What is the start point? What is the stop point?
<--- Score

45. What are the compelling stakeholder reasons for embarking on Public Health Advisor?
<--- Score

46. Is the team equipped with available and reliable resources?
<--- Score

47. How and when will the baselines be defined?
<--- Score

48. How do you gather requirements?
<--- Score

49. Is there a Public Health Advisor management charter, including stakeholder case, problem and goal statements, scope, milestones, roles and responsibilities, communication plan?
<--- Score

50. What constraints exist that might impact the team?
<--- Score

51. When is/was the Public Health Advisor start date?
<--- Score

52. What would be the goal or target for a Public Health Advisor's improvement team?
<--- Score

53. Does the information (if compromised) constitute a violation of regulatory requirements (e.g., FERPA, HIPAA, PIP Act) or organization policy?
<--- Score

54. How do you manage unclear Public Health Advisor requirements?

<--- Score

55. Are customer(s) identified and segmented according to their different needs and requirements?

<--- Score

56. Is there a list of all procedures required by the HIPAA Privacy Rule?

<--- Score

57. What sort of initial information to gather?

<--- Score

58. Encryption requirements: Is the PII encrypted?

<--- Score

59. What is out-of-scope initially?

<--- Score

60. What are the Roles and Responsibilities for each team member and its leadership? Where is this documented?

<--- Score

61. What customer feedback methods were used to solicit their input?

<--- Score

62. What scope do you want your strategy to cover?

<--- Score

63. When is the estimated completion date?

<--- Score

64. How does the case management for long-term mentally ill individuals affect use of health care services?

<--- Score

65. Is there a completed SIPOC representation, describing the Suppliers, Inputs, Process, Outputs, and Customers?

<--- Score

66. How did your organizations administrative offices interact with government/regulatory agencies to satisfy accrediting requirements prior to the initiative(s)?

<--- Score

67. Does this project require a HIPAA-Compliant authorization?

<--- Score

68. Are audit criteria, scope, frequency and methods defined?

<--- Score

69. How often are the team meetings?

<--- Score

70. Has a project plan, Gantt chart, or similar been developed/completed?

<--- Score

71. What critical content must be communicated – who, what, when, where, and how?

<--- Score

72. Is data collected and displayed to better understand customer(s) critical needs and requirements.
<--- Score

73. Has a high-level 'as is' process map been completed, verified and validated?
<--- Score

74. Are improvement team members fully trained on Public Health Advisor?
<--- Score

75. What alternatives for continuing operations of your organization are available in case of loss of any critical function/resource?
<--- Score

76. Is a fully trained team formed, supported, and committed to work on the Public Health Advisor improvements?
<--- Score

77. Are there different segments of customers?
<--- Score

78. Is the current 'as is' process being followed? If not, what are the discrepancies?
<--- Score

79. Is There a Business Case for Quality?
<--- Score

80. Who are the Public Health Advisor improvement team members, including Management Leads and Coaches?

<--- Score

81. Is there a HIPAA requirement?
<--- Score

82. Scope of sensitive information?
<--- Score

83. What are the dynamics of the communication plan?
<--- Score

84. How do you determine veterinary/military public health approval requirements?
<--- Score

85. Who defines (or who defined) the rules and roles?
<--- Score

86. Is the Public Health Advisor scope manageable?
<--- Score

87. What key stakeholder process output measure(s) does Public Health Advisor leverage and how?
<--- Score

88. What specifically is the problem? Where does it occur? When does it occur? What is its extent?
<--- Score

89. Are stakeholder processes mapped?
<--- Score

90. Where can you gather more information?
<--- Score

91. What is in the scope and what is not in scope?
<--- Score

92. Do you have a written policy on protecting public health and the environment through compliance with applicable requirements and conservation programs?
<--- Score

93. Are customers identified and high impact areas defined?
<--- Score

94. How do you hand over Public Health Advisor context?
<--- Score

95. Is the improvement team aware of the different versions of a process: what they think it is vs. what it actually is vs. what it should be vs. what it could be?
<--- Score

96. Have current policies and procedures been compared to HIPAA Privacy requirements?
<--- Score

97. When are meeting minutes sent out? Who is on the distribution list?
<--- Score

98. How does the Public Health Advisor manager ensure against scope creep?
<--- Score

99. What are the core elements of the Public Health Advisor business case?

<--- Score

100. Will team members perform Public Health Advisor work when assigned and in a timely fashion?
<--- Score

101. How will variation in the actual durations of each activity be dealt with to ensure that the expected Public Health Advisor results are met?
<--- Score

Add up total points for this section:
_ _ _ _ _ = Total points for this section

Divided by: _ _ _ _ _ _ (number of statements answered) = _ _ _ _ _ _
Average score for this section

Transfer your score to the Public Health Advisor Index at the beginning of the Self-Assessment.

CRITERION #3: MEASURE:

INTENT: Gather the correct data.
Measure the current performance and
evolution of the situation.

In my belief, the answer to this
question is clearly defined:

5 Strongly Agree

4 Agree

3 Neutral

2 Disagree

1 Strongly Disagree

1. At what cost to privacy?
<--- Score

2. How large is the gap between current performance
and the customer-specified (goal) performance?
<--- Score

**3. Is there a high level of customer andor
stakeholder dissatisfaction with the process**

(quality, timeliness, cost)?
<--- Score

4. Are rules being enforced to remove access by staff members who no longer have a need to know because they have changed assignments or have stopped working for the organization?
<--- Score

5. Are indirect costs charged to the Public Health Advisor program?
<--- Score

6. Who is involved in verifying compliance?
<--- Score

7. Why focus on quality improvement?
<--- Score

8. How do you focus on what is right -not who is right?
<--- Score

9. How do you verify and develop ideas and innovations?
<--- Score

10. Are key measures identified and agreed upon?
<--- Score

11. Are the Public Health Advisor benefits worth its costs?
<--- Score

12. Is it possible to estimate the impact of unanticipated complexity such as wrong or failed

assumptions, feedback, etc. on proposed reforms?
<--- Score

13. How will you measure your progress?
<--- Score

14. What charts has the team used to display the components of variation in the process?
<--- Score

15. What are the key input variables? What are the key process variables? What are the key output variables?
<--- Score

16. Do you use data analysis and objectives to make improvements?
<--- Score

17. Can you measure the return on analysis?
<--- Score

18. What measurements are possible, practicable and meaningful?
<--- Score

19. If technology (e.g., network, server, devices) directly impact safety and health care, how (and by whom) is this information exchanged?
<--- Score

20. If the incremental labor costs are zero, what about capital costs required for such improvements?
<--- Score

21. Is a solid data collection plan established that

includes measurement systems analysis?

<--- Score

22. What is the Impact of Health Care Reform on ASCs and Group Practices?

<--- Score

23. Are you able to realize any cost savings?

<--- Score

24. What impact does the ACT program have on member health care experience?

<--- Score

25. Does each project have a privacy impact?

<--- Score

26. What kind of an impact does the move to Electronic Health Records have on HIPAA privacy and security?

<--- Score

27. How can you measure the performance?

<--- Score

28. Have you made security and privacy a priority?

<--- Score

29. What will it cost to implement the available methods in your environment?

<--- Score

30. Are there any additional costs for COBRA or HIPAA administration?

<--- Score

31. How do you weigh cost savings, delivery, functionality, process improvement, quality, and risk into vendor selection criteria (front vs. back end)?
<--- Score

32. How will costs be allocated?
<--- Score

33. How does measurement fit into health behavior, health education, and public health?
<--- Score

34. Have all non-recommended alternatives been analyzed in sufficient detail?
<--- Score

35. What disadvantage does this cause for the user?
<--- Score

36. What improvement actions correct the root causes to meet customer requirements again?
<--- Score

37. Is data collected on key measures that were identified?
<--- Score

38. Are there competing Public Health Advisor priorities?
<--- Score

39. Why Perform a Privacy Impact Analysis?
<--- Score

40. What data was collected (past, present, future/

ongoing)?
<--- Score

41. Has your organization stated its goals in measurable terms, such as cost, quality, and timeliness?
<--- Score

42. How do you verify the Public Health Advisor requirements quality?
<--- Score

43. What is the potential public health impact?
<--- Score

44. What is your cost benefit analysis?
<--- Score

45. What indicators (quality, cost, time, etc.) are used for each core process?
<--- Score

46. How does the focus of public health practitioners differ from health care providers?
<--- Score

47. What are your key Public Health Advisor organizational performance measures, including key short and longer-term financial measures?
<--- Score

48. Have you found any 'ground fruit' or 'low-hanging fruit' for immediate remedies to the gap in performance?
<--- Score

49. What are the costs and benefits?
<--- Score

50. What has the team done to assure the stability and accuracy of the measurement process?
<--- Score

51. What is the Public Health Impact?
<--- Score

52. Are process variation components displayed/ communicated using suitable charts, graphs, plots?
<--- Score

53. What key measures identified indicate the performance of the stakeholder process?
<--- Score

54. What methods are feasible and acceptable to estimate the impact of reforms?
<--- Score

55. How does a government shutdown impact Public Health Service (PHS) Officers?
<--- Score

56. How can you manage cost down?
<--- Score

57. How do you measure lifecycle phases?
<--- Score

58. The approach of traditional Public Health Advisor works for detail complexity but is focused on a systematic approach rather than an understanding of the nature of systems themselves, what approach

will permit your organization to deal with the kind of unpredictable emergent behaviors that dynamic complexity can introduce?
<--- Score

59. Does alcohol advertising have an impact on public health?
<--- Score

60. What particular quality tools did the team find helpful in establishing measurements?
<--- Score

61. How will you measure your Public Health Advisor effectiveness?
<--- Score

62. Can you make an impact in 8-12 weeks?
<--- Score

63. Is key measure data collection planned and executed, process variation displayed and communicated and performance baselined?
<--- Score

64. Who participated in the data collection for measurements?
<--- Score

65. Do you have any cost Public Health Advisor limitation requirements?
<--- Score

66. What causes mismanagement?
<--- Score

67. What are the current costs of the Public Health Advisor process?
<--- Score

68. Calculate the total cost of ownership to the organization - not just the initial sticker price. Are there any hidden or extra fees?
<--- Score

69. What does your operating model cost?
<--- Score

70. Do improvement programs help in the assessment of quality costs?
<--- Score

71. Where can you go to verify the info?
<--- Score

72. What causes extra work or rework?
<--- Score

73. Are the community coalitions focused on one issue or a broader public health campaign?
<--- Score

74. What are the Public Health Advisor key cost drivers?
<--- Score

75. How do you control the overall costs of your work processes?
<--- Score

76. What are the costs of reform?
<--- Score

77. Who should conduct a privacy impact assessment?

<--- Score

78. Have efforts been made to minimize the negative impacts of the public health measures?

<--- Score

79. How do you verify performance?

<--- Score

80. What evidence is there and what is measured?

<--- Score

81. Has the team clearly expressed the quantitative and qualitative benefits in mission or program improvement terms (e.g., changes in quality, cost, speed, accuracy, or productivity)?

<--- Score

82. What causes innovation to fail or succeed in your organization?

<--- Score

83. Which stakeholder characteristics are analyzed?

<--- Score

84. Is the cost worth the Public Health Advisor effort ?

<--- Score

85. Is a privacy impact assessment mandatory?

<--- Score

86. Is there a high level of customer and/or stakeholder dissatisfaction with the process

(quality, timeliness, cost)?
<--- Score

87. What causes investor action?
<--- Score

88. How are you verifying it?
<--- Score

89. What are the agreed upon definitions of the high impact areas, defect(s), unit(s), and opportunities that will figure into the process capability metrics?
<--- Score

90. How can a Public Health Advisor test verify your ideas or assumptions?
<--- Score

91. What happens if cost savings do not materialize?
<--- Score

92. Are actual costs in line with budgeted costs?
<--- Score

93. How will measures be used to manage and adapt?
<--- Score

94. What are the training priorities in terms of content and audience?
<--- Score

95. How does your organization oversee and promote cybersecurity priorities and share information?
<--- Score

96. Is Process Variation Displayed/Communicated?
<--- Score

97. Is a public health system impact statement required or applicable?
<--- Score

98. Are high impact defects defined and identified in the stakeholder process?
<--- Score

99. What is the cost of your public health program?
<--- Score

100. Is there a Performance Baseline?
<--- Score

101. How do you measure privacy?
<--- Score

102. What are your measureable goals?
<--- Score

103. How might public health impacts interact with climate impacts?
<--- Score

104. How is the value delivered by Public Health Advisor being measured?
<--- Score

105. How often will data be analyzed?
<--- Score

106. What are the root causes of the problem?
<--- Score

107. What are the existing finance/cost-sharing models for public health?
<--- Score

108. Do the benefits outweigh the costs?
<--- Score

109. What is the PII confidentiality impact level?
<--- Score

110. How do you know that any Public Health Advisor analysis is complete and comprehensive?
<--- Score

111. State legislators work on public health-related issues: what influences priorities?
<--- Score

112. Have you assessed the potential savings on health care costs and the effect on the wellness and morale of your workforce by using robots to relieve tedious or potentially deleterious tasks?
<--- Score

113. What relevant entities could be measured?
<--- Score

114. Can you do Public Health Advisor without complex (expensive) analysis?
<--- Score

115. Is a follow-up focused external Public Health Advisor review required?
<--- Score

116. How frequently do you track Public Health Advisor measures?

<--- Score

117. How do you continue to support historical analysis and statistical queries without incurring privacy breaches?

<--- Score

118. Is long term and short term variability accounted for?

<--- Score

119. Is data collection planned and executed?

<--- Score

120. How sensitive must the Public Health Advisor strategy be to cost?

<--- Score

121. Do you verify that corrective actions were taken?

<--- Score

122. Where is it measured?

<--- Score

123. When a disaster occurs, who gets priority?

<--- Score

124. Cost of security or data privacy vulnerability?

<--- Score

125. How do you maintain your organizational focus on performance improvement?

<--- Score

126. Was a data collection plan established?
<--- Score

127. Why is tobacco a public health priority?
<--- Score

128. What indicator(s) of success will you measure?
<--- Score

Add up total points for this section:
_ _ _ _ _ = Total points for this section

Divided by: _ _ _ _ _ _ (number of
statements answered) = _ _ _ _ _ _
Average score for this section

Transfer your score to the Public Health
Advisor Index at the beginning of the
Self-Assessment.

CRITERION #4: ANALYZE:

INTENT: Analyze causes, assumptions and hypotheses.

In my belief, the answer to this question is clearly defined:

5 Strongly Agree

4 Agree

3 Neutral

2 Disagree

1 Strongly Disagree

1. Was a detailed process map created to amplify critical steps of the 'as is' stakeholder process?
<--- Score

2. What does the data say about the performance of the stakeholder process?
<--- Score

3. Do you have a comprehensive data-sharing program in which others share information

about patterns, and use that information to operationalize strategies and close gaps in responses and services?

<--- Score

4. How can the data subject ask to "be forgotten"?

<--- Score

5. What processes do you believe are best suited to promoting safety and quality in nursing and health care settings?

<--- Score

6. Do you, as a leader, bounce back quickly from setbacks?

<--- Score

7. What are your outputs?

<--- Score

8. What is the cost of poor quality as supported by the team's analysis?

<--- Score

9. How will data be displayed?

<--- Score

10. What about Data Subjects under the age of 16?

<--- Score

11. Is the required Public Health Advisor data gathered?

<--- Score

12. Who regulates/controls wording of the Consent for personal data processing document?

<--- Score

13. What are the best opportunities for value improvement?
<--- Score

14. Is your data covered by a privacy policy?
<--- Score

15. Is there a document available online which lists everything that is considered personal data?
<--- Score

16. Are all team members qualified for all tasks?
<--- Score

17. Do you have a quality improvement process?
<--- Score

18. Who is involved with workflow mapping?
<--- Score

19. How do you protect your data and your privacy?
<--- Score

20. Where are the opportunities for improvement that can strengthen the public health system?
<--- Score

21. Is Data Protection covered in the Master Service Agreement?
<--- Score

22. Have all processes and data flows been documented?

<--- Score

23. Describe/list any ongoing quality improvement programs in place. Do you perform internal audits of your billing and claims submission process?
<--- Score

24. Where is data stored (what type of media)?
<--- Score

25. What did the team gain from developing a sub-process map?
<--- Score

26. Do your data reports confirm this is a challenge at your organization?
<--- Score

27. What are evaluation criteria for the output?
<--- Score

28. What are your security and data privacy policies?
<--- Score

29. Do you have a process to delete data if demanded?
<--- Score

30. Were there any improvement opportunities identified from the process analysis?
<--- Score

31. What is the role of a hospital in a new community environment that provides more efficient and effective health care (e.g., what

are the redesigned structures and models, the role and implementation of accountable care organizations, the structures and processes needed to implement new payment models such as bundled payments, and how do organizations transition to this new role)?

<--- Score

32. How often will data be reported?

<--- Score

33. Is baseline data available?

<--- Score

34. What are the options for disposing of data on hardware?

<--- Score

35. Have any additional benefits been identified that will result from closing all or most of the gaps?

<--- Score

36. What about personal data I want to transfer outside the EU or to international organisations?

<--- Score

37. Has a privacy officer evaluated whether the data has been de-identified with respect to HIPAA and other regulations?

<--- Score

38. What if my organization manages data that is governed by statutes like HIPAA?

<--- Score

39. What is your organizations system for selecting

qualified vendors?

<--- Score

40. What are the personnel training and qualifications required?

<--- Score

41. Data Privacy-Who owns the data?

<--- Score

42. What fail-safe measures do you need to ensure your data is protected from a security breach?

<--- Score

43. How often will data be collected?

<--- Score

44. The right to data portability is complimentary - is a bank obliged to provide me with information free of charge?

<--- Score

45. How do you manage recommendations and opportunities for improvement?

<--- Score

46. How do you enhance existing cache management techniques for context-dependent data?

<--- Score

47. How Much Privacy for Your Data?

<--- Score

48. Were any designed experiments used to generate additional insight into the data analysis?

<--- Score

49. What does a controller need to do when it relies on data processors?
<--- Score

50. Does my business need to appoint a Data Protection Officer (DPO)?
<--- Score

51. Are Public Health Advisor changes recognized early enough to be approved through the regular process?
<--- Score

52. Which public health or behavioral health registry do you commonly submit data to?
<--- Score

53. Is the gap/opportunity displayed and communicated in financial terms?
<--- Score

54. What qualifications are necessary?
<--- Score

55. Does the model lead to improvements in quality and process of care?
<--- Score

56. What are the key things I should consider when handling personal data?
<--- Score

57. What legal liabilities exist related to the type of information stored, such as PII or Health Insurance

Portability and Accountability Act (HIPAA)-protected data?

<--- Score

58. How does your organization determine its key health care processes process requirements and design these processes to meet all the key requirements including staff safety?

<--- Score

59. Are some process problems of greater public health significance?

<--- Score

60. What are obligations for Data Processors?

<--- Score

61. What constitutes personal data?

<--- Score

62. What Public Health Advisor metrics are outputs of the process?

<--- Score

63. When data is Modified, processed, or exchanged (transmitted to other systems, applications, users) effective audit records are generated?

<--- Score

64. Do you have existing data (baseline and target)?

<--- Score

65. What is this data telling us?

<--- Score

66. Do data processors need 'explicit' or 'unambiguous' data subject consent - and what is the difference?
<--- Score

67. Do your contracts/agreements contain data security obligations?
<--- Score

68. Does your organization have data to demonstrate a trend of three years or more worth of improvements in quality or service and / or product by all of your major suppliers?
<--- Score

69. What is your organizations process which leads to recognition of value generation?
<--- Score

70. Did any additional data need to be collected?
<--- Score

71. What are the necessary qualifications?
<--- Score

72. What are the revised rough estimates of the financial savings/opportunity for Public Health Advisor improvements?
<--- Score

73. What non-public health use of the data are required or allowed by law?
<--- Score

74. What tools were used to narrow the list of possible

causes?

<--- Score

75. What is the Value Stream Mapping?

<--- Score

76. How is business process management similar to quality improvement approaches such as total quality management?

<--- Score

77. What were the financial benefits resulting from any 'ground fruit or low-hanging fruit' (quick fixes)?

<--- Score

78. What process improvements and reviews will be necessary?

<--- Score

79. Is the performance gap determined?

<--- Score

80. Who is responsible for the overall audit process and results?

<--- Score

81. What tools were used to generate the list of possible causes?

<--- Score

82. How do you ensure Information integrity (e.g., quality control process, transaction and output reconstruction)?

<--- Score

83. What mechanisms are implemented to assess

the effectiveness of the audit process (metrics)?
<--- Score

84. Big data and privacy: what is the big deal?
<--- Score

85. Is the Public Health Advisor process severely broken such that a re-design is necessary?
<--- Score

86. How often will data be collected for measures?
<--- Score

87. What are your best practices for minimizing Public Health Advisor project risk, while demonstrating incremental value and quick wins throughout the Public Health Advisor project lifecycle?
<--- Score

88. Was a cause-and-effect diagram used to explore the different types of causes (or sources of variation)?
<--- Score

89. Can institutions and investigators subject to the Federal Health Insurance Privacy and Portability Act (HIPAA) Privacy Rule share data in accord with the NIH Data Sharing policy?
<--- Score

90. Think about the functions involved in your Public Health Advisor project, what processes flow from these functions?
<--- Score

91. Does your organization follow Six Sigma or Lean Sigma quality methodologies for process

improvement?

<--- Score

92. What changes will drive your progress ?

<--- Score

93. Do you have a process to provide data to individuals who ask?

<--- Score

94. How was the detailed process map generated, verified, and validated?

<--- Score

95. Can the consent for personal data processing be granted to us over the phone?

<--- Score

96. When do data mining results violate privacy?

<--- Score

97. How does the vendor handle data privacy?

<--- Score

98. How much data control and privacy is required?

<--- Score

99. Can you meet data privacy rules?

<--- Score

100. Do you know where your data is today?

<--- Score

101. How will the system and processes in five years time protect and enhance public health?

<--- Score

102. Cycle time - do you have data that shows that wait times are long?
<--- Score

103. Have the problem and goal statements been updated to reflect the additional knowledge gained from the analyze phase?
<--- Score

104. Are target agreements for continual improvement of products and processes made and implemented with the supplier base?
<--- Score

105. What about privacy and data protection?
<--- Score

106. Are you able to answer a regulator asking "where did you get the data and how did the data subject agree to it being collected?"
<--- Score

107. What data is maintained by your organization, and where?
<--- Score

108. Where can you get qualified talent today?
<--- Score

109. Were Pareto charts (or similar) used to portray the 'heavy hitters' (or key sources of variation)?
<--- Score

110. What conclusions were drawn from the team's

data collection and analysis? How did the team reach these conclusions?

<--- Score

111. Are you transferring data overseas?

<--- Score

112. Without data governance, how do data improvement opportunities traditionally become known to it?

<--- Score

113. Did any value-added analysis or 'lean thinking' take place to identify some of the gaps shown on the 'as is' process map?

<--- Score

114. Does the process map influence the outcome of quality improvement work?

<--- Score

115. Is the final output clearly identified?

<--- Score

116. Does HIPAA apply to all identifiable health data?

<--- Score

117. What training and qualifications will you need?

<--- Score

118. Are the processes stable and reliable?

<--- Score

119. Is data collection necessary to respond to a public health emergency?

<--- Score

120. Will the GDPR set up a one-stop-shop for data privacy regulation?
<--- Score

121. Does your organization have a distinct quality program that support continuous process improvement?
<--- Score

122. Are your outputs consistent?
<--- Score

123. Does the supplier have a Continuous Improvement Process they apply to processes and products?
<--- Score

124. Will research data be placed in the medical record?
<--- Score

125. How is Public Health Advisor data gathered?
<--- Score

126. Is data and process analysis, root cause analysis and quantifying the gap/opportunity in place?
<--- Score

127. SHOULD WE UPDATE THE INFORMATION GIVEN TO DATA SUBJECTS?
<--- Score

128. What were the crucial 'moments of truth' on the process map?

<--- Score

129. Is employee attendance also considered to be personal data?

<--- Score

130. Data subjects can demand that their data be deleted; do you have a process for this when asked?

<--- Score

131. What quality tools were used to get through the analyze phase?

<--- Score

132. Privacy: who owns the data?

<--- Score

133. Total quality management. six sigma. eight omega. iso 9000. cmm. bpmm. scor. The number of process improvement frameworks out there is staggering. which ones do you incorporate?

<--- Score

134. Based on what you know, how do hospitals and integrated health care delivery systems (IDSs) use IHIE data and reports to improve medical care?

<--- Score

135. Are gaps between current performance and the goal performance identified?

<--- Score

136. What data is gathered?

<--- Score

137. Is any confidential (pci, pii, HIPAA, other) data stored in the database?

<--- Score

138. You have defined data gathering (who/how/when/integrity of data) using The 7 Step Improvement Process

<--- Score

139. What mechanisms will be implemented to assess the effectiveness of the review process (measures)?

<--- Score

Add up total points for this section:
_ _ _ _ _ = Total points for this section

Divided by: _ _ _ _ _ _ (number of statements answered) = _ _ _ _ _ _
Average score for this section

Transfer your score to the Public Health Advisor Index at the beginning of the Self-Assessment.

CRITERION #5: IMPROVE:

INTENT: Develop a practical solution. Innovate, establish and test the solution and to measure the results.

In my belief, the answer to this question is clearly defined:

5 Strongly Agree

4 Agree

3 Neutral

2 Disagree

1 Strongly Disagree

1. Have the types of information and uses of that information been identified and the sensitivity of each type of information been evaluated?
<--- Score

2. Are quality and safety measured for the purpose of ongoing improvement?
<--- Score

3. How do you demonstrate commitment to quality education and quality improvement?

<--- Score

4. Policy makers: what are the facts and statistics related to public health risk?

<--- Score

5. Is there a high likelihood that any recommendations will achieve their intended results?

<--- Score

6. What were the key strategies or ingredients in place that likely led to improvement on the quality indicators?

<--- Score

7. Quality Improvement Education is Provided?

<--- Score

8. How do you improve productivity?

<--- Score

9. Describe the design of the pilot and what tests were conducted, if any?

<--- Score

10. Are you reaching your ultimate result?

<--- Score

11. From a public health perspective, what are the key risks?

<--- Score

12. How does the brain or the senses work differently during groupthink, are there

measurable results in improvement?
<--- Score

13. What actions can be taken to mitigate risk?
<--- Score

14. Is the solution technically practical?
<--- Score

15. Do urban regeneration programs improve public health and reduce health inequalities?
<--- Score

16. Was a pilot designed for the proposed solution(s)?
<--- Score

17. What is effective to improve public health and public safety?
<--- Score

18. Are there any constraints (technical, political, cultural, or otherwise) that would inhibit certain solutions?
<--- Score

19. Who gets results on specimens submitted to the public health lab?
<--- Score

20. How do the review findings inform improvements in the organisation?
<--- Score

21. Quality improvement: what steps are taken to ensure continuous quality improvement?
<--- Score

22. Who will make public health decisions?

<--- Score

23. Do you use management reviews to make improvements?

<--- Score

24. How can you recognize continuous quality improvement?

<--- Score

25. What do you think are the most important ingredients necessary for improving quality, and for establishing successful QI initiatives?

<--- Score

26. How will you document the decisions and actions?

<--- Score

27. What changes can you make that will result in improvement?

<--- Score

28. What is the implementation plan?

<--- Score

29. What are the barriers to successful quality improvement?

<--- Score

30. Are improvements done as a result of the product measurements effective in improving product quality?

<--- Score

31. What is your vision for your Quality Improvement culture?
<--- Score

32. Who do you report Public Health Advisor results to?
<--- Score

33. How does your organization start its development of a QI program?
<--- Score

34. Why were qi initiatives developed?
<--- Score

35. Is there a cost/benefit analysis of optimal solution(s)?
<--- Score

36. What is quality improvement?
<--- Score

37. How does the solution remove the key sources of issues discovered in the analyze phase?
<--- Score

38. Who are the people involved in developing and implementing Public Health Advisor?
<--- Score

39. What is the magnitude of the improvements?
<--- Score

40. Are changes designed to improve one part of the system causing new problems in other parts of

the system?
<--- Score

41. What is quality improvement ?
<--- Score

42. Are new and improved process ('should be') maps developed?
<--- Score

43. Who has the authority to decide whether you are eligible for VA health care?
<--- Score

44. Are the best solutions selected?
<--- Score

45. Is there a small-scale pilot for proposed improvement(s)? What conclusions were drawn from the outcomes of a pilot?
<--- Score

46. Risk factors: what are the characteristics of Public Health Advisor that make it risky?
<--- Score

47. Do you document or report your organization s progress?
<--- Score

48. What are milestones and markers on the roadmap to the main outcomes?
<--- Score

49. Are you working on any quality improvement projects?

<--- Score

50. Do you currently use any Quality Improvement Tools?
<--- Score

51. Does the goal represent a desired result that can be measured?
<--- Score

52. How will you know when its improved?
<--- Score

53. Do you know your organizations product delivery & improvement goals and what you must do to support them?
<--- Score

54. If you could go back in time five years, what decision would you make differently? What is your best guess as to what decision you're making today you might regret five years from now?
<--- Score

55. How does a quality assurance professional manage an engineered strategy to counter the quality impediments and develop a quality improvement initiative?
<--- Score

56. How do you measure risk?
<--- Score

57. What resources are required for the improvement efforts?
<--- Score

58. What is the budget for external services to assist with an evaluation?

<--- Score

59. How is evidence defined and evaluated within a public health context?

<--- Score

60. You know where you are on the QI Road map and where should you be in one year?

<--- Score

61. How do you assure ongoing improvement of your quality system?

<--- Score

62. Will the project improve public health and safety?

<--- Score

63. What does the 'should be' process map/design look like?

<--- Score

64. How can you improve performance?

<--- Score

65. Satisfaction surveys or team brainstorms - what improvement project should you be working on?

<--- Score

66. Are improved process ('should be') maps modified based on pilot data and analysis?

<--- Score

67. How do you make improvements?
<--- Score

68. What tools were used to tap into the creativity and encourage 'outside the box' thinking?
<--- Score

69. What service level measures will you use to account for new service delivery method and commitments for improvements in quality and efficiency?
<--- Score

70. What needs improvement? Why?
<--- Score

71. How does your organization address continuous quality improvement?
<--- Score

72. How can manufacturing improvement techniques such as lean and Six Sigma be used to improve quality in your automated laboratories?
<--- Score

73. How will the team or the process owner(s) monitor the implementation plan to see that it is working as intended?
<--- Score

74. What is the budget for internal resources to assist with an evaluation?
<--- Score

75. How can e-health improve access to health

care?

<--- Score

76. What challenges do you foresee occurring in the future in the effort to continue to improve quality?

<--- Score

77. What are the implications of the one critical Public Health Advisor decision 10 minutes, 10 months, and 10 years from now?

<--- Score

78. What changes can you make that will result in an improvement?

<--- Score

79. What lessons, if any, from a pilot were incorporated into the design of the full-scale solution?

<--- Score

80. Do you combine technical expertise with business knowledge and Public Health Advisor Key topics include lifecycles, development approaches, requirements and how to make a business case?

<--- Score

81. In what ways, if any, was the CFO involved in quality improvement measures?

<--- Score

82. Why does not Human Resources just decide who can have access to various categories of PHI by job title?

<--- Score

83. What error proofing will be done to address some of the discrepancies observed in the 'as is' process?
<--- Score

84. Who are the key stakeholders for the evaluation?
<--- Score

85. Does pay-for-performance improve the quality of health care?
<--- Score

86. Are possible solutions generated and tested?
<--- Score

87. How were quality goals and strategies developed?
<--- Score

88. Were any criteria developed to assist the team in testing and evaluating potential solutions?
<--- Score

89. What is your organizations quality improvement and how does/will it transform healthcare?
<--- Score

90. Have public health response decisions been made in a clear, open, and transparent manner?
<--- Score

91. What is Public Health Advisor's impact on utilizing the best solution(s)?
<--- Score

92. What do auditors expect to see for public health measure documentation?

<--- Score

93. What is the objective (projected improvement to the CTQ)?

<--- Score

94. Is management supporting your organizational culture that encourages continuous improvement?

<--- Score

95. Is pilot data collected and analyzed?
<--- Score

96. How can qi models be leveraged to accomplish improvements effectively and efficiently?
<--- Score

97. How will you know that a change is an improvement?
<--- Score

98. How do you keep improving Public Health Advisor?
<--- Score

99. What were the underlying assumptions on the cost-benefit analysis?
<--- Score

100. Are all required policies and procedures documented?
<--- Score

101. Is the optimal solution selected based on testing and analysis?
<--- Score

102. What tools were used to evaluate the potential solutions?
<--- Score

103. How will the group know that the solution worked?
<--- Score

104. Does any event pose a threat to the routine safety and sanitary environments for travellers, or constitute a public health risk at designated ports of entry?
<--- Score

105. In what geographies is public health improving?
<--- Score

106. At what point will vulnerability assessments be performed once Public Health Advisor is put into production (e.g., ongoing Risk Management after implementation)?
<--- Score

107. How risky is your organization?
<--- Score

108. What are the improvement goals for next cycle / project?
<--- Score

109. Are the assets/ threats/ risks/ safeguards

being dictated by HIPAA XE HIPAA ?

<--- Score

110. Is a contingency plan established?

<--- Score

111. What is the team's contingency plan for potential problems occurring in implementation?

<--- Score

112. What are key operational risks that could result in a breach of security?

<--- Score

113. What is health care quality and who decides?

<--- Score

114. Is the scope clearly documented?

<--- Score

115. What were the major barriers faced in developing and implementing QI efforts?

<--- Score

116. Have QI efforts led to improvements or declines in the financial health of the institution?

<--- Score

117. Among the top improvers in quality, what forces or events motivated them to seriously address quality issues?

<--- Score

118. What resources are required for the improvement?

<--- Score

119. How will you know that you have improved?
<--- Score

120. Is a solution implementation plan established, including schedule/work breakdown structure, resources, risk management plan, cost/budget, and control plan?
<--- Score

121. What tools were most useful during the improve phase?
<--- Score

122. Can you mitigate risk by anticipating a potential problem?
<--- Score

123. Which of the recognised risks out of all risks can be most likely transferred?
<--- Score

124. Who is responsible for conducting the risk assessment?
<--- Score

125. Risk events: what are the things that could go wrong?
<--- Score

126. Are there any Total Quality Management or Continuous Improvement initiatives in operation?
<--- Score

127. What tools do you use once you have decided on a Public Health Advisor strategy and more

importantly how do you choose?
<--- Score

128. Is the implementation plan designed?
<--- Score

129. What if members of the health care team disagree regarding a capacity assessment, who has the final authority to make this decision?
<--- Score

130. What communications are necessary to support the implementation of the solution?
<--- Score

131. What attendant changes will need to be made to ensure that the solution is successful?
<--- Score

132. Are risk triggers captured?
<--- Score

133. How did the team generate the list of possible solutions?
<--- Score

134. Does it include a commitment to continual improvement of the QMS?
<--- Score

135. Do improvement projects need to be done with an interprofessional team?
<--- Score

136. What is a public health risk?
<--- Score

137. How do you change an existing culture to one where it is a Quality Improvement culture?
<--- Score

138. From a public health perspective what are the key risks?
<--- Score

Add up total points for this section:
_____ = Total points for this section

Divided by: _____ (number of statements answered) = _____
Average score for this section

Transfer your score to the Public Health Advisor Index at the beginning of the Self-Assessment.

CRITERION #6: CONTROL:

INTENT: Implement the practical solution. Maintain the performance and correct possible complications.

In my belief, the answer to this question is clearly defined:

5 Strongly Agree

4 Agree

3 Neutral

2 Disagree

1 Strongly Disagree

1. This program provides Quality Assurance Productivity Improvement in Work, Standardization, Accuracy-First-Time?
<--- Score

2. Have you been told your organization needs to comply with certain information privacy and/or security standards, such as PCI, HIPAA, etc.?
<--- Score

3. How can you best use all of your knowledge repositories to enhance learning and sharing?
<--- Score

4. Does the response plan contain a definite closed loop continual improvement scheme (e.g., plan-do-check-act)?
<--- Score

5. How will input, process, and output variables be checked to detect for sub-optimal conditions?
<--- Score

6. Do your organizations IT systems have the capacity to set access controls?
<--- Score

7. What other systems, operations, processes, and infrastructures (hiring practices, staffing, training, incentives/rewards, metrics/dashboards/scorecards, etc.) need updates, additions, changes, or deletions in order to facilitate knowledge transfer and improvements?
<--- Score

8. How is the plan to be tested?
<--- Score

9. You may have created your quality measures at a time when you lacked resources, technology wasn't up to the required standard, or low service levels were the industry norm. Have those circumstances changed?
<--- Score

10. Is a response plan in place for when the input, process, or output measures indicate an 'out-of-control' condition?
<--- Score

11. Should public health surveillance be used as a monitoring tool?
<--- Score

12. Are there documented procedures?
<--- Score

13. How will new or emerging customer needs/requirements be checked/communicated to orient the process toward meeting the new specifications and continually reducing variation?
<--- Score

14. What are your results for key measures or indicators of the accomplishment of your Public Health Advisor strategy and action plans, including building and strengthening core competencies?
<--- Score

15. Does the Public Health Advisor performance meet the customer's requirements?
<--- Score

16. Will your goals reflect your program budget?
<--- Score

17. Will any special training be provided for results interpretation?
<--- Score

18. How will the process owner verify improvement in

present and future sigma levels, process capabilities?
<--- Score

19. What is the backup plan for access to the facility and systems?
<--- Score

20. Have new or revised work instructions resulted?
<--- Score

21. Is there a formal (documented) system security plan?
<--- Score

22. How will report readings be checked to effectively monitor performance?
<--- Score

23. Are the planned controls working?
<--- Score

24. Have security controls been specified for the business associate?
<--- Score

25. Does job training on the documented procedures need to be part of the process team's education and training?
<--- Score

26. Are new process steps, standards, and documentation ingrained into normal operations?
<--- Score

27. Are processes to achieve continual improvement of the quality management system

planned and managed?

<--- Score

28. Is reporting being used or needed?

<--- Score

29. Do labor safety and health care facilities conform to the standards set by your organization?

<--- Score

30. Is new knowledge gained imbedded in the response plan?

<--- Score

31. How do you spread information?

<--- Score

32. How widespread is its use?

<--- Score

33. Is there a recommended audit plan for routine surveillance inspections of Public Health Advisor's gains?

<--- Score

34. Do policies reflect public health science and current practice standards?

<--- Score

35. What is the plan to revise the review process when needed?

<--- Score

36. How do you encourage people to take control and responsibility?

<--- Score

37. Do you have a Quality Improvement or Quality Assurance Plan?
<--- Score

38. How does your qa plan measure areas of opportunities for improvement?
<--- Score

39. How do senior leaders actions reflect a commitment to the organizations Public Health Advisor values?
<--- Score

40. What are the critical parameters to watch?
<--- Score

41. Is there a standardized process?
<--- Score

42. Does it provide Quality Assurance Productivity Improvement in CAD Work, Standardization, Accuracy-First-Time?
<--- Score

43. Is there a control plan in place for sustaining improvements (short and long-term)?
<--- Score

44. Are documented procedures clear and easy to follow for the operators?
<--- Score

45. Who is going to spread your message?
<--- Score

46. Does a troubleshooting guide exist or is it needed?
<--- Score

47. Who is responsible for the contingency plan?
<--- Score

48. Are suggested corrective/restorative actions indicated on the response plan for known causes to problems that might surface?
<--- Score

49. Is a response plan established and deployed?
<--- Score

50. How do controls support value?
<--- Score

51. How do your controls stack up?
<--- Score

52. Is there a plan for improvement or future development that encompasses high quality dementia care?
<--- Score

53. Do you have privacy controls for communications?
<--- Score

54. Have you established a HIPAA test environment, team, coordinator, plan?
<--- Score

55. Besides HIPAA, what external compliance rules must organizations consider when planning

security?
<--- Score

56. What are the key elements of your Public Health Advisor performance improvement system, including your evaluation, organizational learning, and innovation processes?
<--- Score

57. Are the parts/steps in the system performing as planned?
<--- Score

58. Is there documentation that will support the successful operation of the improvement?
<--- Score

59. How will the process owner and team be able to hold the gains?
<--- Score

60. Is there a documented and implemented monitoring plan?
<--- Score

61. What should the next improvement project be that is related to Public Health Advisor?
<--- Score

62. How will you know if your plan is working?
<--- Score

63. When Does the ISO 9000 Quality Assurance Standard Lead to Performance Improvement?
<--- Score

64. Privacy should not be an afterthought; a bolt-on sometime between the initial coding and delivery of a new system. It should be designed in from the start; peer-reviewed; tested and the data controller needs to be able to show that adequate security is in place; it is monitored; and that the strictest data protection policies will apply by default. If you design your own custom apps; are these the standards you work to? When deploying purchased systems; is privacy set at its tightest by default?
<--- Score

65. Who controls critical resources?
<--- Score

66. Did you do what you planned to do?
<--- Score

67. What motivates people to improve (improvement plan, quality objectives)?
<--- Score

68. Is this data de-identified according to HIPAA privacy standards as a matter of course?
<--- Score

69. What are you attempting to measure/monitor?
<--- Score

70. Who is the Public Health Advisor process owner?
<--- Score

71. Is there a local emergency/public health plan?
<--- Score

72. How do you plan on providing proper recognition and disclosure of supporting companies?

<--- Score

73. How do you exploit twitter for public health monitoring?

<--- Score

74. Has a labor safety and health care system been established and perfected, with the labor safety and health care regulations and standards of your organization strictly implemented?

<--- Score

75. Can HIPAA and cognate state laws harmonize to promote optimal standards for data collection, use, analysis, and encryption?

<--- Score

76. How might the group capture best practices and lessons learned so as to leverage improvements?

<--- Score

77. What is the control/monitoring plan?

<--- Score

78. What key inputs and outputs are being measured on an ongoing basis?

<--- Score

79. What is the recommended frequency of auditing?

<--- Score

80. How is your cybersecurity incident/breach response plan audited?

<--- Score

81. How will you measure your QA plan's effectiveness?

<--- Score

82. Which Quality Standards and areas of improvement require long-term solutions?

<--- Score

83. Is knowledge gained on process shared and institutionalized?

<--- Score

84. What other areas of the group might benefit from the Public Health Advisor team's improvements, knowledge, and learning?

<--- Score

85. Are operating procedures consistent?

<--- Score

86. What is the plan to revise the audit process when needed?

<--- Score

87. Are your processes mission critical like regulatory compliance standards that require full visibility and traceability of every action and decision within a process such as: PCI, HIPAA and SOX?

<--- Score

88. Is there a transfer of ownership and knowledge to process owner and process team tasked with the responsibilities.

<--- Score

89. Are there policies and procedures related to the security of access controls?

<--- Score

90. Why should a public health department build a Quality Improvement (QI) Plan?

<--- Score

91. How is Public Health Advisor project cost planned, managed, monitored?

<--- Score

92. Has the improved process and its steps been standardized?

<--- Score

93. How will the day-to-day responsibilities for monitoring and continual improvement be transferred from the improvement team to the process owner?

<--- Score

94. Does monitoring in fact leads to improvements in your organizations activities?

<--- Score

95. Is there a link between quality standards and performance improvement?

<--- Score

96. What motivates people to improve (improvement plan, quality objectives and standards)?

<--- Score

97. When does ISO 9000 quality assurance standard lead to performance improvements?

<--- Score

98. Which Quality Standards and areas of improvement can be addressed immediately?

<--- Score

99. Do you monitor the effectiveness of your Public Health Advisor activities?

<--- Score

100. What is your quality improvement plan?

<--- Score

101. What quality tools were useful in the control phase?

<--- Score

102. If penetration testing has been determined to be reasonable and appropriate, has specifically worded, written approval from senior management been received for any planned penetration testing?

<--- Score

Add up total points for this section:
_____ = Total points for this section

Divided by: _____ (number of statements answered) = _____
Average score for this section

Transfer your score to the Public Health Advisor Index at the beginning of the Self-Assessment.

CRITERION #7: SUSTAIN:

INTENT: Retain the benefits.

In my belief, the answer to this question is clearly defined:

5 Strongly Agree

4 Agree

3 Neutral

2 Disagree

1 Strongly Disagree

1. How is access to the PII determined?
<--- Score

2. Have QI initiatives affected the institutions competitiveness in the market?
<--- Score

3. Does your organization have procedures to ensure compliance with HIPAA?
<--- Score

4. What is a Public Health Emergency?
<--- Score

5. How will the HITRUST threat catalogue help you with HIPAA compliance?
<--- Score

6. Is there a procedure in place for reporting and handling incidents?
<--- Score

7. Have you implemented a Privacy Policy?
<--- Score

8. What is your Privacy Policy?
<--- Score

9. Are all key stakeholders present at all Structured Walkthroughs?
<--- Score

10. Do you think Public Health Advisor accomplishes the goals you expect it to accomplish?
<--- Score

11. What is the empirical basis for paying for quality in health care?
<--- Score

12. Has implementation been effective in reaching specified objectives so far?
<--- Score

13. What outcomes are desired?
<--- Score

14. What are your organizations challenges in providing quality services and supports?

<--- Score

15. How does transportation affect public health?

<--- Score

16. Is there an ongoing QI program that provides feedback with specifics about CPR performance to EMTs following every cardiac arrest?

<--- Score

17. Do you have privacy manager?

<--- Score

18. Do you have designated Privacy Officers?

<--- Score

19. How do you know if you are successful?

<--- Score

20. How much does Public Health Advisor help?

<--- Score

21. Do you have the ability to deliver this consistently at all levels of the organization?

<--- Score

22. What is unique about the public health system and structure?

<--- Score

23. Is access to health care a right for all?

<--- Score

24. What is the public health significance of

Epigenetics?
<--- Score

25. Who is responsible for privacy?
<--- Score

26. What is your vision of Your QI culture?
<--- Score

27. Have staff members been made aware of the identity and roles of supervisors?
<--- Score

28. What are the challenges in training public health leaders in the country/region?
<--- Score

29. What does your signature ensure?
<--- Score

30. What should a proof of concept or pilot accomplish?
<--- Score

31. Is there a procedure in place to ensure that everyone in your organization receives security awareness training?
<--- Score

32. What are the primary public health goals for your organization?
<--- Score

33. Were lessons learned captured and communicated?
<--- Score

34. What knowledge, skills and characteristics mark a good Public Health Advisor project manager?
<--- Score

35. Do Public Health Advisor rules make a reasonable demand on a users capabilities?
<--- Score

36. What do you stand for--and what are you against?
<--- Score

37. How can you negotiate Public Health Advisor successfully with a stubborn boss, an irate client, or a deceitful coworker?
<--- Score

38. Do you have a flow diagram of what happens?
<--- Score

39. What is the overall business strategy?
<--- Score

40. How do you foster the skills, knowledge, talents, attributes, and characteristics you want to have?
<--- Score

41. Is there any work affecting public health or safety?
<--- Score

42. Where do Privacy filters get implemented?
<--- Score

43. Who should receive life support during a public health emergency?

<--- Score

44. What is initial file(s) where PII was collected?
<--- Score

45. Have employees been trained on security?
<--- Score

46. Security: will cybersecurity overwhelm privacy?
<--- Score

47. Who is responsible for ensuring appropriate resources (time, people and money) are allocated to Public Health Advisor?
<--- Score

48. Does the regulatory system really add to public health?
<--- Score

49. Times a week to review the status of each individual - can meetings be held by HIPAA compliant video chat?
<--- Score

50. Are Designers Ready for Privacy by Design?
<--- Score

51. What is (and is not) privacy?
<--- Score

52. What health systems will succeed in such a reformed health care landscape?
<--- Score

53. Do you have systems in place to distribute public health organization information to community organizations?

<--- Score

54. Does your organization review privacy notices?

<--- Score

55. What is the message to deliver to the rest of the organization on what is QI in your organization?

<--- Score

56. Security: will cyber security overwhelm privacy?

<--- Score

57. For what purpose is PII used?

<--- Score

58. Who else should you help?

<--- Score

59. Are you paying enough attention to the partners your company depends on to succeed?

<--- Score

60. Do you have the necessary buy-in and leadership support?

<--- Score

61. What is qi in public health?

<--- Score

62. Which incidents / trend represent a serious public health threat?

<--- Score

63. Does the exposure contain pii?
<--- Score

64. What are your predictions as to what will happen?
<--- Score

65. Can communities and academia work together on public health research?
<--- Score

66. Does the website have a posted privacy notice?
<--- Score

67. What final/delivery files contain PII?
<--- Score

68. What are the challenges?
<--- Score

69. Is social power a determinant of public health?
<--- Score

70. Do you pay attention to HIPAA?
<--- Score

71. What have you done to protect your business from competitive encroachment?
<--- Score

72. Does the vendor have a Privacy Program?
<--- Score

73. What significant public health services are provided by other organizations?

<--- Score

74. Is Public Health Advisor dependent on the successful delivery of a current project?
<--- Score

75. Is there a goal or target?
<--- Score

76. Is there a public health threat?
<--- Score

77. Who have you, as a company, historically been when you've been at your best?
<--- Score

78. For what primary purpose is PII used?
<--- Score

79. What might be a serious threat to public health or safety?
<--- Score

80. What have been your experiences in defining long range Public Health Advisor goals?
<--- Score

81. Who cares about IT Security and Privacy?
<--- Score

82. Is your Institution, or any part of it, covered by HIPAA?
<--- Score

83. To whom do you communicate with at your local public health or emergency management

organization?

<--- Score

84. Do you have the resources to devote to this to make it a reality?

<--- Score

85. Are there any privacy concerns?

<--- Score

86. Who communicates an alert to your local public health or emergency management organization?

<--- Score

87. What qi approaches are used in public health?

<--- Score

88. Are you changing as fast as the world around you?

<--- Score

89. Is the cloud ferpa, HIPAA, and fisma compliant?

<--- Score

90. Are new benefits received and understood?

<--- Score

91. What is an appropriate level of privacy?

<--- Score

92. In a project to restructure Public Health Advisor outcomes, which stakeholders would you involve?

<--- Score

93. Is your organization subject to HIPAA?

<--- Score

94. If no one would ever find out about your accomplishments, how would you lead differently?
<--- Score

95. What are your HIPAA goals?
<--- Score

96. How can you ensure privacy is protected?
<--- Score

97. Who should be responsible for privacy - the CSPs?
<--- Score

98. How does Public Health Advisor integrate with other stakeholder initiatives?
<--- Score

99. What kind of outcome could be anticipated?
<--- Score

100. For HIPAA, glba and/or other state or federal regulation compliance, what due diligence/ auditing is performed to ensure that you remain in compliance and what individual(s) in your organization are responsible for said compliance?
<--- Score

101. Can you look up information about your spouse or family member?
<--- Score

102. Who has primary responsibility for protecting ePHI?
<--- Score

103. Is the HIPAA privacy rule suspended during a national or public health emergency?
<--- Score

104. Who and what department was responsible for oversight of this program?
<--- Score

105. How do you minimize your use of sensitive PII?
<--- Score

106. Does it support your core values?
<--- Score

107. How much money is at stake?
<--- Score

108. Do you have past Public Health Advisor successes?
<--- Score

109. How do you know when you are finished?
<--- Score

110. Where is public health education going in the next 5 to 10 years?
<--- Score

111. What is the intended use of the PII collected?
<--- Score

112. What goals did you miss?
<--- Score

113. What types of information does HIPAA protect?

<--- Score

114. What are the Privacy principles for HealthVault?

<--- Score

115. Are there any security or privacy concerns?

<--- Score

116. Do you have the will to do this throughout the organization?

<--- Score

117. How do you state a privacy policy?

<--- Score

118. Why is Public Health Advisor important for you now?

<--- Score

119. What other health care professionals do you interact with regularly?

<--- Score

120. Are there consequences for failure to comply?

<--- Score

121. Is the pii shared with other organizations?

<--- Score

122. Do you feel that ADR reporting can benefit the public health?

<--- Score

123. How is the program funded - does it compete for resources with other programs?

<--- Score

124. What Are the Key Privacy Concerns in the Cloud?

<--- Score

125. Does your organization comply with HIPAA?

<--- Score

126. At what point is privacy violated?

<--- Score

127. Is there a crosswalk listing of HITRUST with the other frameworks such as HIPAA, FISMA, PCI, ISO, etc. that you can provide?

<--- Score

128. What technology barriers may arise in the technology adoption associated with artificial intelligence for your organization?

<--- Score

129. What is the source for PII collected?

<--- Score

130. Do you have an implicit bias for capital investments over people investments?

<--- Score

131. Does the public health organization have a role in the managed care environment?

<--- Score

132. Privacy options?

<--- Score

133. Privacy notices: are privacy policies useful?
<--- Score

134. Virtual Teams can be to health care delivery, as 3D printing will become to manufacturing?
<--- Score

135. Will you administer HIPAA and assure compliance with HIPAA law?
<--- Score

136. Who is on the team?
<--- Score

137. How can legacy decommissioning systems be made more resilient?
<--- Score

138. Does Office 365 allow customers to be HIPAA/ HITECH Act compliant?
<--- Score

139. Do you see more potential in people than they do in themselves?
<--- Score

140. What is the difference between a HIPAA and a HITRUST assessment?
<--- Score

141. What is the starting point to assess gaps between the supply and demand of health care providers?
<--- Score

142. Why is storytelling a job for public health?
<--- Score

143. What business benefits will Public Health Advisor goals deliver if achieved?
<--- Score

144. Have QI efforts or other initiatives you have discussed led to changes in your quality indicators?
<--- Score

145. At what moment would you think; Will I get fired?
<--- Score

146. Is the activity dispersed among programs or only addressed in one area of public health?
<--- Score

147. What is consumer engagement in health care?
<--- Score

148. What is a Substantial and Specific Danger to Public Health or Safety?
<--- Score

149. Does testing lend itself to a phased approach?
<--- Score

150. Do members of the team have the authority to speak for your organization to the media, law enforcement, and clients or business partners?
<--- Score

151. Ask yourself: how would you do this work if you

only had one staff member to do it?
<--- Score

152. How many individuals PII is in the system?
<--- Score

153. How do you manage Public Health Advisor Knowledge Management (KM)?
<--- Score

154. Is there a potential for a real threat to public health and/or the environment?
<--- Score

155. What Public Health Advisor skills are most important?
<--- Score

156. How much contingency will be available in the budget?
<--- Score

157. Who are four people whose careers you have enhanced?
<--- Score

158. Which models, tools and techniques are necessary?
<--- Score

159. Is there a variation in public health benefit for different populations?
<--- Score

160. What information in the system is PII?
<--- Score

161. What strategies/systems were used, if any, to hold staff accountable for their roles in making QI initiatives successful?

<--- Score

162. What is the best tool app for creating a digital signature?

<--- Score

163. Are policies and procedures in place for security?

<--- Score

164. How has technology changed privacy?

<--- Score

165. Can greenwashing also pose a threat to the environment and even to public health?

<--- Score

166. What Are the Benefits of Integrated Health Care?

<--- Score

167. Are you using a design thinking approach and integrating Innovation, Public Health Advisor Experience, and Brand Value?

<--- Score

168. How will you know that the Public Health Advisor project has been successful?

<--- Score

169. What if you receive a request for PHI on your pager?

<--- Score

170. Is there any reason to believe the opposite of my current belief?
<--- Score

171. Is any pii shared with other organizations?
<--- Score

172. What services do Public Health commission?
<--- Score

173. What are the unintended consequences of HIPAA?
<--- Score

174. What are the short and long-term Public Health Advisor goals?
<--- Score

175. What is the significance of information systems for health care?
<--- Score

176. How have you tracked changes in quality and/or efficiency over the course of these initiatives being in place?
<--- Score

177. Marketing budgets are tighter, consumers are more skeptical, and social media has changed forever the way we talk about Public Health Advisor. How do you gain traction?
<--- Score

178. Who has access to pii / phi over the web

portal?
<--- Score

179. For whom (or for what system)?
<--- Score

180. How many principles for public health ethics?
<--- Score

181. Is subject to mandated protection under HIPAA, ferpa, or other federal or state statutes?
<--- Score

182. Who on your team is responsible for privacy?
<--- Score

183. How does your system maintain privacy and ensure HIPAA compliancy?
<--- Score

184. Who Is Responsible for Protecting Privacy?
<--- Score

185. What must you excel at?
<--- Score

186. How is privacy and security managed with IoT?
<--- Score

187. Have benefits been optimized with all key stakeholders?
<--- Score

188. Can you make it easy to do the right thing?
<--- Score

189. How should public health informatics proceed in this age of Electronic Health Records and the Affordable Care Act?

<--- Score

190. Have new benefits been realized?
<--- Score

191. Do you have the right people on the bus?
<--- Score

192. What do you want to achieve?
<--- Score

193. Are the right players on your team?
<--- Score

194. What Is Privacy?
<--- Score

195. What Public Health Advisor modifications can you make work for you?
<--- Score

196. Are labor safety and health care facilities for new, re-building or expansion projects designed, constructed and put into use simultaneously with the main projects?
<--- Score

197. How do you keep the momentum going?
<--- Score

198. Is consumer privacy respected?
<--- Score

199. Do you use terms that are understood by a non-public health audience?

<--- Score

200. How do you build new formats for behavior change communication to propel public health information?

<--- Score

201. Is there any flexibility on beginning new public health approaches earlier?

<--- Score

202. Do you have adequate privacy?

<--- Score

203. Regional health information organizations: a vehicle for transforming health care delivery?

<--- Score

204. What factors affect access to health care?

<--- Score

205. How many suppliers with access to PII?

<--- Score

206. Do you have adequate privacy laws?

<--- Score

207. How do you set Public Health Advisor stretch targets and how do you get people to not only participate in setting these stretch targets but also that they strive to achieve these?

<--- Score

208. Were concrete goals or benchmarks established?

<--- Score

209. Is the impact that Public Health Advisor has shown?
<--- Score

210. Who are the key stakeholders?
<--- Score

211. What is your message to the organization on what QI will be in your organization?

<--- Score

212. What intermediate files contain PII?

<--- Score

213. How are you protecting privacy?

<--- Score

214. What challenges exist in compiling evidence for public health practice?

<--- Score

215. Is the legacy system HIPAA compliant?

<--- Score

216. What types of PII are obtained?

<--- Score

217. How do you engage the workforce, in addition to satisfying them?
<--- Score

218. Are You Covered under HIPAA?

<--- Score

219. What environmental tests does your public health lab perform?

<--- Score

220. How likely is it that a customer would recommend your company to a friend or colleague?

<--- Score

221. How much security/privacy?

<--- Score

222. What tools are in place?

<--- Score

223. What do we do when new problems arise?

<--- Score

224. What management system can you use to leverage the Public Health Advisor experience, ideas, and concerns of the people closest to the work to be done?

<--- Score

225. Have you been able to obtain HIPAA-related information?

<--- Score

226. What are the success criteria that will indicate that Public Health Advisor objectives have been met and the benefits delivered?

<--- Score

227. Surveillance is a key function of public health, and what does it mean?

<--- Score

228. Does a measurable public health goal exist?
<--- Score

229. What are the key enablers to make this Public Health Advisor move?
<--- Score

230. Based on the readings over the last several weeks, what are the key challenges that you face as a health care professional in the future?
<--- Score

231. What is the Vision for the Health and Health Care Delivery System?
<--- Score

232. What is the local public health departments role in a field investigation?
<--- Score

233. Who uses your product in ways you never expected?
<--- Score

234. How will you align with other public health efforts?
<--- Score

235. Do employees know whom to contact and how to handle a security incident?
<--- Score

236. Recap: Why is privacy preserved?
<--- Score

237. What is the best way to set up a private HIPAA compliant server for your organization?
<--- Score

238. Can pseudonymity really guarantee privacy?
<--- Score

239. How do you assess the Public Health Advisor pitfalls that are inherent in implementing it?
<--- Score

240. Are you / should you be revolutionary or evolutionary?
<--- Score

241. Is privacy implemented into design?
<--- Score

242. What is the source for the PII collected?
<--- Score

243. Are privacy & reasonable personal use compatible?
<--- Score

244. Who must comply with the HIPAA rules?
<--- Score

245. Where does the QI department rank in the institutions hierarchy?
<--- Score

246. Where do new ideas come from?
<--- Score

247. Do policies and procedures already exist regarding access to and use of facilities and equipment?

<--- Score

248. Can you Assure Confidentiality In Health Care Services For Adolescents And Young Adults?

<--- Score

249. If your customer were your grandmother, would you tell her to buy what you're selling?

<--- Score

250. Who reports privacy matters to the Board?

<--- Score

251. Is there such a thing as too much care?

<--- Score

252. Does this support the mission and vision of your organization?

<--- Score

253. Who within your organization is responsible for complying with HIPAA?

<--- Score

254. What PII will be collected?

<--- Score

255. How would healthier people benefit from Public Health and Health Care?

<--- Score

256. Can electronic medical record systems transform health care?

<--- Score

257. Do you think you know, or do you know you know ?
<--- Score

258. Who will step in to maintain the public health?
<--- Score

259. Is it HIPAA compliant?
<--- Score

260. Do you know the privacy laws?
<--- Score

261. Who do we want your customers to become?
<--- Score

262. Is there assurance that information is not altered during transmission?
<--- Score

263. How do public health professionals know when a program is working?
<--- Score

264. What is the overall talent health of your organization as a whole at senior levels, and for each organization reporting to a member of the Senior Leadership Team?
<--- Score

265. Who do you want your customers to become?
<--- Score

266. What questions is it raising?

<--- Score

267. What are the customer privacy policies?

<--- Score

268. Do you use the HIPAA Security Rule Framework?

<--- Score

269. Do you make information regularly available to managers, staff, and others?

<--- Score

270. Is privacy by design enough?

<--- Score

271. Does privacy compete with fair use?

<--- Score

272. What will the privacy implications be?

<--- Score

273. What is Privacy by Design?

<--- Score

274. How effectively has your organization reached out to other health care settings to coordinate care for clients with complex illnesses?

<--- Score

275. How are you training the public health workforce?

<--- Score

276. How can you become the company that would

put you out of business?
<--- Score

277. What partnerships with public health or medical professionals are currently in place?
<--- Score

278. If you had to leave your organization for a year and the only communication you could have with employees/colleagues was a single paragraph, what would you write?
<--- Score

279. How do customers see your organization?
<--- Score

280. What you are going to do to affect the numbers?
<--- Score

281. How can I protect the privacy of my subjects?
<--- Score

282. Are polarized privacy screens installed?
<--- Score

283. What are you looking for in terms of public health experience and training?
<--- Score

284. Who are your customers?
<--- Score

285. Do you hire local staff members that have graduated from other public health programs?
<--- Score

286. What is your formula for success in Public Health Advisor ?

<--- Score

287. Would you rather sell to knowledgeable and informed customers or to uninformed customers?

<--- Score

288. How is privacy maintained?

<--- Score

289. How do you maintain Public Health Advisor's Integrity?

<--- Score

290. What is the purpose of your Privacy Policy?

<--- Score

291. Are the workforce competencies predictive of essential service performance?

<--- Score

292. Have employees received a copy of, and do they have ready access to, your organizations security procedures and policies?

<--- Score

293. How do you communicate your public health message?

<--- Score

294. How will the PII be secured?

<--- Score

295. What is the appropriate role of interprofessional education in public health?

<--- Score

296. Does each app have a privacy/security policy?
<--- Score

297. Classification: How and when is PII classified?
<--- Score

298. How engaged are consumers in their health and health care, and why does it matter?
<--- Score

299. What design choices were made to enhance privacy?
<--- Score

300. Do you know who is a friend or a foe?
<--- Score

301. What may be the consequences for the performance of an organization if all stakeholders are not consulted regarding Public Health Advisor?
<--- Score

302. Is Public Health Advisor realistic, or are you setting yourself up for failure?
<--- Score

303. What do you expect of managers and front line staff?
<--- Score

304. Is there an inventory of facilities and existing security practices?
<--- Score

305. Have you translated public health and jargon into laymans terms?

<--- Score

306. Do you have a written privacy or security policy?

<--- Score

307. Are public health authorities considered business associates?

<--- Score

308. Who, on the executive team or the board, has spoken to a customer recently?

<--- Score

309. Are there any other things of which health care providers should be made aware?

<--- Score

310. How do you deal with Public Health Advisor changes?

<--- Score

311. Does HIPAA apply to HealthVault accounts?

<--- Score

312. Are you affected by HIPAA?

<--- Score

313. What long-term trajectory are public health supply chains taking?

<--- Score

314. Can the schedule be done in the given time?

<--- Score

315. What are some good choices for HIPAA compliant cloud storage?
<--- Score

316. Will quality remodeling affect obstetrician-gynecologists in addition to clients?
<--- Score

317. Has labor safety and health care education been conducted among the workers?
<--- Score

318. Do you have a current HIPAA (health information privacy & security) Compliance Program in place?
<--- Score

319. Do you have a privacy policy?
<--- Score

320. How do you lead with Public Health Advisor in mind?
<--- Score

321. How can organizations of Public Health provide surge capacity?
<--- Score

322. Integrated Delivery Networks: A Detour on the Road to Integrated Health Care?
<--- Score

323. Is access to PII necessary to achieve a specified public health function?
<--- Score

324. A decade after 9/11, are we better prepared for public health emergencies?

<--- Score

325. What is the kind of project structure that would be appropriate for your Public Health Advisor project, should it be formal and complex, or can it be less formal and relatively simple?

<--- Score

326. Does a Public Health Advisor quantification method exist?

<--- Score

327. What, specifically, is the public health approach to youth violence?

<--- Score

328. Procedures exist to track the media externally?

<--- Score

329. What, if any, support is provided by external providers (Internet service providers ISPs, utilities, or contractors)?

<--- Score

330. Does your organization have a HIPAA privacy training program?

<--- Score

331. How do you ensure your compliance with HIPAA, PCI, etc.?

<--- Score

Add up total points for this section:
_____ = Total points for this section

Divided by: _____ (number of
statements answered) = _____
Average score for this section

Transfer your score to the Public Health
Advisor Index at the beginning of the
Self-Assessment.

Public Health Advisor and Managing Projects, Criteria for Project Managers:

1.0 Initiating Process Group: Public Health Advisor

1. What are the overarching issues of your organization?

2. Do you understand all business (operational), technical, resource and vendor risks associated with the Public Health Advisor project?

3. How do you help others satisfy needs?

4. What are the pressing issues of the hour?

5. What will you do to minimize the impact should a risk event occur?

6. When will the Public Health Advisor project be done?

7. How well did you do?

8. What were things that you did well, and could improve, and how?

9. How well defined and documented were the Public Health Advisor project management processes you chose to use?

10. Specific - is the objective clear in terms of what, how, when, and where the situation will be changed?

11. What are the constraints?

12. What is the stake of others in your Public Health

Advisor project?

13. What must be done?

14. Did the Public Health Advisor project team have the right skills?

15. How can you make your needs known?

16. During which stage of Risk planning are risks prioritized based on probability and impact?

17. Are stakeholders properly informed about the status of the Public Health Advisor project?

18. Based on your Public Health Advisor project communication management plan, what worked well?

19. Were resources available as planned?

20. What areas does the group agree are the biggest success on the Public Health Advisor project?

1.1 Project Charter: Public Health Advisor

21. Is it an improvement over existing products?

22. Name and describe the elements that deal with providing the detail?

23. Customer benefits: what customer requirements does this Public Health Advisor project address?

24. How will you know that a change is an improvement?

25. Pop quiz – which are the same inputs as in the Public Health Advisor project charter?

26. Public Health Advisor project deliverables: what is the Public Health Advisor project going to produce?

27. Environmental stewardship and sustainability considerations: what is the process that will be used to ensure compliance with the environmental stewardship policy?

28. Strategic fit: what is the strategic initiative identifier for this Public Health Advisor project?

29. How will you learn more about the process or system you are trying to improve?

30. Did your Public Health Advisor project ask for this?

31. Does the Public Health Advisor project need to consider any special capacity or capability issues?

32. Where does all this information come from?

33. Public Health Advisor project objective statement: what must the Public Health Advisor project do?

34. When?

35. What are the assumptions?

36. What metrics could you look at?

37. Why executive support?

38. Market – identify products market, including whether it is outside of the objective: what is the purpose of the program or Public Health Advisor project?

39. What are the assigned resources?

1.2 Stakeholder Register: Public Health Advisor

40. How will reports be created?

41. What is the power of the stakeholder?

42. Who wants to talk about Security?

43. Who is managing stakeholder engagement?

44. Who are the stakeholders?

45. How much influence do they have on the Public Health Advisor project?

46. How big is the gap?

47. What are the major Public Health Advisor project milestones requiring communications or providing communications opportunities?

48. Is your organization ready for change?

49. What opportunities exist to provide communications?

50. What & Why?

51. How should employers make voices heard?

1.3 Stakeholder Analysis Matrix: Public Health Advisor

52. Arena: in what fields are the actors active, where are they present?

53. Accreditations, qualifications, certifications?

54. Is there evidence that demonstrates the impact of education on the Public Health Advisor projects outcomes?

55. What is social & public accountability ?

56. Competitor intentions - various?

57. How can you fill the need to show progress?

58. Resources, assets, people?

59. How are the threatened Public Health Advisor project targets being used?

60. Who are potential allies and opponents?

61. Partnerships, agencies, distribution?

62. Accreditations, etc?

63. Opponents; who are the opponents?

64. What is your Advocacy Strategy?

65. Is there a reason why you are or are not not using an external rating system?

66. Technology development and innovation?

67. Processes and systems, etc?

68. What mechanisms are proposed to monitor and measure Public Health Advisor project performance in terms of social development outcomes?

69. Are you working on the right risks?

70. Which resources are required?

71. Market developments?

2.0 Planning Process Group: Public Health Advisor

72. How will it affect you?

73. What is involved in Public Health Advisor project scope management, and why is good Public Health Advisor project scope management so important on information technology Public Health Advisor projects?

74. Are there efficient coordination mechanisms to avoid overloading the counterparts, participating stakeholders?

75. What is a Software Development Life Cycle (SDLC)?

76. How does activity resource estimation affect activity duration estimation?

77. Product breakdown structure (pbs): what is the Public Health Advisor project result or product, and how should it look like, what are its parts?

78. To what extent is the program helping to influence your organizations policy framework?

79. When developing the estimates for Public Health Advisor project phases, you choose to add the individual estimates for the activities that comprise each phase. What type of estimation method are you using?

80. How are it Public Health Advisor projects different?

81. Contingency planning. if a risk event occurs, what will you do?

82. To what extent and in what ways are the Public Health Advisor project contributing to progress towards organizational reform?

83. What good practices or successful experiences or transferable examples have been identified?

84. Public Health Advisor project assessment; why did you do this Public Health Advisor project?

85. To what extent are the participating departments coordinating with each other?

86. How can you tell when you are done?

87. In what ways can the governance of the Public Health Advisor project be improved so that it has greater likelihood of achieving future sustainability?

88. In which Public Health Advisor project management process group is the detailed Public Health Advisor project budget created?

89. In what way has the Public Health Advisor project come up with innovative measures for problem-solving?

90. Are work methodologies, financial instruments, etc. shared among departments, organizations and Public Health Advisor projects?

2.1 Project Management Plan: Public Health Advisor

91. Are the existing and future without-plan conditions reasonable and appropriate?

92. What are the deliverables?

93. What went right?

94. Why Change?

95. How do you manage integration?

96. What data/reports/tools/etc. do your PMs need?

97. If the Public Health Advisor project is complex or scope is specialized, do you have appropriate and/or qualified staff available to perform the tasks?

98. Did the planning effort collaborate to develop solutions that integrate expertise, policies, programs, and Public Health Advisor projects across entities?

99. What is risk management?

100. Why do you manage integration?

101. What went wrong?

102. Who is the Public Health Advisor project Manager?

103. How do you manage time?

104. What are the training needs?

105. If the Public Health Advisor project management plan is a comprehensive document that guides you in Public Health Advisor project execution and control, then what should it NOT contain?

106. What is Public Health Advisor project scope management?

107. What is the justification?

108. Does the selected plan protect privacy?

2.2 Scope Management Plan: Public Health Advisor

109. Is there a scope management plan that includes how Public Health Advisor project scope will be defined, developed, monitored, validated and controlled?

110. Are decisions captured in a decisions log?

111. Has the selected plan been formulated using cost effectiveness and incremental analysis techniques?

112. Describe the manner in which Public Health Advisor project deliverables will be formally presented and accepted. Will they be presented at the end of each phase?

113. Why do you need to manage scope?

114. Materials available for performing the work?

115. Are measurements and feedback mechanisms incorporated in tracking work effort & refining work estimating techniques?

116. Has a capability assessment been conducted?

117. Are the schedule estimates reasonable given the Public Health Advisor project?

118. What are the risks that could significantly affect the budget of the Public Health Advisor project?

119. Has a resource management plan been created?

120. Has a structured approach been used to break work effort into manageable components (WBS)?

121. Has stakeholder analysis been conducted, assessing influence on the Public Health Advisor project and authority levels?

122. Are software metrics formally captured, analyzed and used as a basis for other Public Health Advisor project estimates?

123. Would the Public Health Advisor project cost sharing involve reimbursement to the sponsor?

124. Who is doing what for whom?

125. What is the most common tool for helping define the detail?

126. Where do scope management processes fit in?

127. Are action items captured and managed?

128. Are you spending the right amount of money for specific tasks?

2.3 Requirements Management Plan: Public Health Advisor

129. Who will initially review the Public Health Advisor project work or products to ensure it meets the applicable acceptance criteria?

130. Is the system software (non-operating system) new to the IT Public Health Advisor project team?

131. How do you know that you have done this right?

132. Will you have access to stakeholders when you need them?

133. Will you perform a Requirements Risk assessment and develop a plan to deal with risks?

134. How detailed should the Public Health Advisor project get?

135. How often will the reporting occur?

136. Who will approve the requirements (and if multiple approvers, in what order)?

137. Do you have price sheets and a methodology for determining the total proposal cost?

138. What performance metrics will be used?

139. Should you include sub-activities?

140. Is it new or replacing an existing business system or process?

141. Did you provide clear and concise specifications?

142. Does the Public Health Advisor project have a Change Control process?

143. Is requirements work dependent on any other specific Public Health Advisor project or non-Public Health Advisor project activities (e.g. funding, approvals, procurement)?

144. Will you use an assessment of the Public Health Advisor project environment as a tool to discover risk to the requirements process?

145. Have stakeholders been instructed in the Change Control process?

146. When and how will a requirements baseline be established in this Public Health Advisor project?

147. Is the change control process documented?

148. How will you develop the schedule of requirements activities?

2.4 Requirements Documentation: Public Health Advisor

149. What kind of entity is a problem ?

150. Where do system and software requirements come from, what are sources?

151. How to document system requirements?

152. What are the acceptance criteria?

153. Who is involved?

154. How much testing do you need to do to prove that your system is safe?

155. How does what is being described meet the business need?

156. If applicable; are there issues linked with the fact that this is an offshore Public Health Advisor project?

157. What are the attributes of a customer?

158. How can you document system requirements?

159. Is your business case still valid?

160. Does the system provide the functions which best support the customers needs?

161. What marketing channels do you want to use:

e-mail, letter or sms?

162. The problem with gathering requirements is right there in the word gathering. What images does it conjure?

163. Is the requirement properly understood?

164. Is new technology needed?

165. How do you know when a Requirement is accurate enough?

166. Completeness. are all functions required by the customer included?

167. Can you check system requirements?

168. What if the system wasn t implemented?

2.5 Requirements Traceability Matrix: Public Health Advisor

169. How do you manage scope?

170. Do you have a clear understanding of all subcontracts in place?

171. Describe the process for approving requirements so they can be added to the traceability matrix and Public Health Advisor project work can be performed. Will the Public Health Advisor project requirements become approved in writing?

172. What percentage of Public Health Advisor projects are producing traceability matrices between requirements and other work products?

173. What are the chronologies, contingencies, consequences, criteria?

174. What is the WBS?

175. Why use a WBS?

176. Will you use a Requirements Traceability Matrix?

177. Why do you manage scope?

178. How small is small enough?

179. How will it affect the stakeholders personally in their career?

180. Is there a requirements traceability process in place?

2.6 Project Scope Statement: Public Health Advisor

181. Will all tasks resulting from issues be entered into the Public Health Advisor project Plan and tracked through the plan?

182. Is the change control process documented and on file?

183. Will this process be communicated to the customer and Public Health Advisor project team?

184. Which risks does the Public Health Advisor project focus on?

185. Is the quality function identified and assigned?

186. Are there adequate Public Health Advisor project control systems?

187. Will the risk documents be filed?

188. Will the qa related information be reported regularly as part of the status reporting mechanisms?

189. Once its defined, what is the stability of the Public Health Advisor project scope?

190. Is the plan for your organization of the Public Health Advisor project resources adequate?

191. Has the Public Health Advisor project scope

statement been reviewed as part of the baseline process?

192. Will the risk plan be updated on a regular and frequent basis?

193. Is there a Change Management Board?

194. Is the Public Health Advisor project manager qualified and experienced in Public Health Advisor project management?

195. Is the plan under configuration management?

196. Will you need a statement of work?

197. Are there issues that could affect the existing requirements for the result, service, or product if the scope changes?

198. If there are vendors, have they signed off on the Public Health Advisor project Plan?

199. Risks?

200. Change management vs. change leadership - what is the difference?

2.7 Assumption and Constraint Log: Public Health Advisor

201. Are there unnecessary steps that are creating bottlenecks and/or causing people to wait?

202. What worked well?

203. What do you log?

204. Have all stakeholders been identified?

205. Are there procedures in place to effectively manage interdependencies with other Public Health Advisor projects / systems?

206. If appropriate, is the deliverable content consistent with current Public Health Advisor project documents and in compliance with the Document Management Plan?

207. Violation trace: why ?

208. Are funding and staffing resource estimates sufficiently detailed and documented for use in planning and tracking the Public Health Advisor project?

209. Is the process working, and people are not executing in compliance of the process?

210. When can log be discarded?

211. Model-building: what data-analytic strategies are useful when building proportional-hazards models?

212. Are there nonconformance issues?

213. Have all necessary approvals been obtained?

214. Do the requirements meet the standards of correctness, completeness, consistency, accuracy, and readability?

215. Contradictory information between document sections?

216. Are there cosmetic errors that hinder readability and comprehension?

217. Are there processes in place to ensure that all the terms and code concepts have been documented consistently?

218. Are requirements management tracking tools and procedures in place?

219. Are best practices and metrics employed to identify issues, progress, performance, etc.?

220. Are you meeting your customers expectations consistently?

2.8 Work Breakdown Structure: Public Health Advisor

221. When would you develop a Work Breakdown Structure?

222. Why would you develop a Work Breakdown Structure?

223. Is it a change in scope?

224. When does it have to be done?

225. Is it still viable?

226. How big is a work-package?

227. How much detail?

228. Where does it take place?

229. Is the work breakdown structure (wbs) defined and is the scope of the Public Health Advisor project clear with assigned deliverable owners?

230. When do you stop?

231. What has to be done?

232. Why is it useful?

233. Can you make it?

234. What is the probability that the Public Health Advisor project duration will exceed xx weeks?

235. What is the probability of completing the Public Health Advisor project in less that xx days?

236. How far down?

237. How many levels?

238. How will you and your Public Health Advisor project team define the Public Health Advisor projects scope and work breakdown structure?

239. Do you need another level?

240. Who has to do it?

2.9 WBS Dictionary: Public Health Advisor

241. Are data elements reconcilable between internal summary reports and reports forwarded to us?

242. Changes in the direct base to which overhead costs are allocated?

243. Is data disseminated to the contractors management timely, accurate, and usable?

244. What is the goal?

245. What are you counting on?

246. Does the contractors system provide unit costs, equivalent unit or lot costs in terms of labor, material, other direct, and indirect costs?

247. Are records maintained to show how management reserves are used?

248. Do the lines of authority for incurring indirect costs correspond to the lines of responsibility for management control of the same components of costs?

249. Incurrence of actual indirect costs in excess of budgets, by element of expense?

250. Is each control account assigned to a single organizational element directly responsible for the

work and identifiable to a single element of the CWBS?

251. Are time-phased budgets established for planning and control of level of effort activity by category of resource; for example, type of manpower and/or material?

252. Is all contract work included in the CWBS?

253. Evaluate the performance of operating organizations?

254. Are procedures established to prevent changes to the contract budget base other than the already stated authorized by contractual action?

255. Are budgets or values assigned to work packages and planning packages in terms of dollars, hours, or other measurable units?

256. Are work packages assigned to performing organizations?

257. Are all affected work authorizations, budgeting, and scheduling documents amended to properly reflect the effects of authorized changes?

258. Appropriate work authorization documents which subdivide the contractual effort and responsibilities, within functional organizations?

2.10 Schedule Management Plan: Public Health Advisor

259. Quality assurance overheads?

260. Are meeting minutes captured and sent out after the meeting?

261. What will be the format of the schedule model?

262. Are milestone deliverables effectively tracked and compared to Public Health Advisor project plan?

263. Has the Public Health Advisor project scope been baselined?

264. Has the scope management document been updated and distributed to help prevent scope creep?

265. Is the development plan and/or process documented?

266. Why conduct schedule analysis?

267. Are Public Health Advisor project team members involved in detailed estimating and scheduling?

268. Who is responsible for estimating the activity resources?

269. What threats might prevent you from getting there?

270. Is the schedule updated on a periodic basis?

271. Are vendor contract reports, reviews and visits conducted periodically?

272. Were Public Health Advisor project team members involved in the development of activity & task decomposition?

273. Does the ims reflect accurate current status and credible start/finish forecasts for all to-go tasks and milestones?

274. Has the ims content been baselined and is it adequately controlled?

275. Staffing Requirements?

276. Are the Public Health Advisor project team members located locally to the users/stakeholders?

277. Does a documented Public Health Advisor project organizational policy & plan (i.e. governance model) exist?

278. Are staff skills known and available for each task?

2.11 Activity List: Public Health Advisor

279. In what sequence?

280. What is your organizations history in doing similar activities?

281. How do you determine the late start (LS) for each activity?

282. What will be performed?

283. How can the Public Health Advisor project be displayed graphically to better visualize the activities?

284. Where will it be performed?

285. Who will perform the work?

286. How detailed should a Public Health Advisor project get?

287. When do the individual activities need to start and finish?

288. How should ongoing costs be monitored to try to keep the Public Health Advisor project within budget?

289. How will it be performed?

290. Is infrastructure setup part of your Public Health Advisor project?

291. For other activities, how much delay can be tolerated?

292. What is the total time required to complete the Public Health Advisor project if no delays occur?

293. Can you determine the activity that must finish, before this activity can start?

294. Is there anything planned that does not need to be here?

2.12 Activity Attributes: Public Health Advisor

295. How difficult will it be to do specific activities on this Public Health Advisor project?

296. Would you consider either of corresponding activities an outlier?

297. What activity do you think you should spend the most time on?

298. Where else does it apply?

299. Can more resources be added?

300. Activity: what is In the Bag?

301. How many days do you need to complete the work scope with a limit of X number of resources?

302. How else could the items be grouped?

303. How difficult will it be to complete specific activities on this Public Health Advisor project?

304. Resource is assigned to?

305. Are the required resources available?

306. Resources to accomplish the work?

307. Which method produces the more accurate cost

assignment?

308. Why?

309. Are the required resources available or need to be acquired?

310. Do you feel very comfortable with your prediction?

311. Were there other ways you could have organized the data to achieve similar results?

2.13 Milestone List: Public Health Advisor

312. Describe the industry you are in and the market growth opportunities. What is the market for your technology, product or service?

313. Effects on core activities, distraction?

314. Sustaining internal capabilities?

315. Sustainable financial backing?

316. Do you foresee any technical risks or developmental challenges?

317. Continuity, supply chain robustness?

318. Political effects?

319. How soon can the activity start?

320. Milestone pages should display the UserID of the person who added the milestone. Does a report or query exist that provides this audit information?

321. Loss of key staff?

322. Describe your organizations strengths and core competencies. What factors will make your organization succeed?

323. Information and research?

324. What has been done so far?

325. How will you get the word out to customers?

326. Legislative effects?

327. What date will the task finish?

328. What specific improvements did you make to the Public Health Advisor project proposal since the previous time?

329. Calculate how long can activity be delayed?

330. Who will manage the Public Health Advisor project on a day-to-day basis?

2.14 Network Diagram: Public Health Advisor

331. What activity must be completed immediately before this activity can start?

332. What is the probability of completing the Public Health Advisor project in less that xx days?

333. What is the lowest cost to complete this Public Health Advisor project in xx weeks?

334. Why must you schedule milestones, such as reviews, throughout the Public Health Advisor project?

335. If the Public Health Advisor project network diagram cannot change and you have extra personnel resources, what is the BEST thing to do?

336. How difficult will it be to do specific activities on this Public Health Advisor project?

337. Are the gantt chart and/or network diagram updated periodically and used to assess the overall Public Health Advisor project timetable?

338. What is the completion time?

339. What activities must follow this activity?

340. If a current contract exists, can you provide the vendor name, contract start, and contract expiration

date?

341. Review the logical flow of the network diagram. Take a look at which activities you have first and then sequence the activities. Do they make sense?

342. What are the Key Success Factors?

343. Where do you schedule uncertainty time?

344. What to do and When?

345. Will crashing x weeks return more in benefits than it costs?

346. Are you on time?

347. What can be done concurrently?

348. What are the Major Administrative Issues?

2.15 Activity Resource Requirements: Public Health Advisor

349. Do you use tools like decomposition and rolling-wave planning to produce the activity list and other outputs?

350. Organizational Applicability?

351. What are constraints that you might find during the Human Resource Planning process?

352. Other support in specific areas?

353. How do you handle petty cash?

354. Are there unresolved issues that need to be addressed?

355. What is the Work Plan Standard?

356. When does monitoring begin?

357. Why do you do that?

358. Time for overtime?

359. How many signatures do you require on a check and does this match what is in your policy and procedures?

360. Which logical relationship does the PDM use most often?

361. Anything else?

2.16 Resource Breakdown Structure: Public Health Advisor

362. How difficult will it be to do specific activities on this Public Health Advisor project?

363. Any changes from stakeholders?

364. When do they need the information?

365. Which resource planning tool provides information on resource responsibility and accountability?

366. What is the purpose of assigning and documenting responsibility?

367. What is each stakeholders desired outcome for the Public Health Advisor project?

368. What is the difference between % Complete and % work?

369. What are the requirements for resource data?

370. What can you do to improve productivity?

371. Why is this important?

372. What defines a successful Public Health Advisor project?

373. Who is allowed to perform which functions?

374. Why time management?

375. Goals for the Public Health Advisor project. What is each stakeholders desired outcome for the Public Health Advisor project?

376. Is predictive resource analysis being done?

377. Who will be used as a Public Health Advisor project team member?

2.17 Activity Duration Estimates: Public Health Advisor

378. What do you think about the WBSs for them?

379. Does a process exist to identify which qualified resources may be attainable?

380. What is the duration of a milestone?

381. Are activity dependencies identified?

382. Are procedures defined by which the Public Health Advisor project scope may be changed?

383. Do your results resemble a normal distribution?

384. Consider the history of modern quality management. How have experts such as Deming, Juran, Crosby, and Taguchi affected the quality movement and todays use of Six Sigma?

385. Which skills do you think are most important for an information technology Public Health Advisor project manager?

386. Is training acquired to enhance the skills, knowledge and capabilities of the Public Health Advisor project team?

387. What are the three main outputs of quality control?

388. Are contingency plans created to prepare for risk events to occur?

389. What do corresponding sources say about Public Health Advisor project management?

390. Are tools and techniques defined for gathering, integrating and distributing Public Health Advisor project outputs?

391. When would a milestone chart be used instead of a bar char?

392. Do procedures exist describing how the Public Health Advisor project scope will be managed?

393. Will the new application be developed using existing hardware, software, and networks?

394. What is the difference between conceptual, application, and evaluative questions?

395. What tasks must precede this task?

396. Who will promote it?

397. Are training needs identified when resources do not have the required skills to complete Public Health Advisor project activities?

2.18 Duration Estimating Worksheet: Public Health Advisor

398. What is next?

399. Is a construction detail attached (to aid in explanation)?

400. Small or large Public Health Advisor project?

401. Does the Public Health Advisor project provide innovative ways for stakeholders to overcome obstacles or deliver better outcomes?

402. Why estimate costs?

403. Can the Public Health Advisor project be constructed as planned?

404. How should ongoing costs be monitored to try to keep the Public Health Advisor project within budget?

405. What is cost and Public Health Advisor project cost management?

406. What is the total time required to complete the Public Health Advisor project if no delays occur?

407. What is an Average Public Health Advisor project?

408. Do any colleagues have experience with your organization and/or RFPs?

409. Science = process: remember the scientific method?

410. What are the critical bottleneck activities?

411. Is the Public Health Advisor project responsive to community need?

412. How can the Public Health Advisor project be displayed graphically to better visualize the activities?

413. What is your role?

414. What info is needed?

415. Why estimate time and cost?

2.19 Project Schedule: Public Health Advisor

416. Are quality inspections and review activities listed in the Public Health Advisor project schedule(s)?

417. Are activities connected because logic dictates the order in which others occur?

418. Are procedures defined by which the Public Health Advisor project schedule may be changed?

419. How much slack is available in the Public Health Advisor project?

420. How do you manage Public Health Advisor project Risk?

421. Why do you think schedule issues often cause the most conflicts on Public Health Advisor projects?

422. Master Public Health Advisor project schedule?

423. How detailed should a Public Health Advisor project get?

424. Why do you need to manage Public Health Advisor project Risk?

425. Have all Public Health Advisor project delays been adequately accounted for, communicated to all stakeholders and adjustments made in overall Public Health Advisor project schedule?

426. What documents, if any, will the subcontractor provide (eg Public Health Advisor project schedule, quality plan etc)?

427. Is Public Health Advisor project work proceeding in accordance with the original Public Health Advisor project schedule?

428. Schedule/cost recovery?

429. Is the structure for tracking the Public Health Advisor project schedule well defined and assigned to a specific individual?

430. Month Public Health Advisor project take?

431. Is there a Schedule Management Plan that establishes the criteria and activities for developing, monitoring and controlling the Public Health Advisor project schedule?

432. Your Public Health Advisor project management plan results in a Public Health Advisor project schedule that is too long. If the Public Health Advisor project network diagram cannot change and you have extra personnel resources, what is the BEST thing to do?

433. What is risk?

434. How effectively were issues able to be resolved without impacting the Public Health Advisor project Schedule or Budget?

2.20 Cost Management Plan: Public Health Advisor

435. Why do you manage cost?

436. Are the people assigned to the Public Health Advisor project sufficiently qualified?

437. Have process improvement efforts been completed before requirements efforts begin?

438. Time management – how will the schedule impact of changes be estimated and approved?

439. Are all resource assumptions documented?

440. Have activity relationships and interdependencies within tasks been adequately identified?

441. Have stakeholder accountabilities & responsibilities been clearly defined?

442. How does the proposed individual meet each requirement?

443. Is there general agreement & acceptance of the current status and progress of the Public Health Advisor project?

444. Who will prepare the cost estimates?

445. Progress measurement and control – How will

the Public Health Advisor project measure and control progress?

446. Are written status reports provided on a designated frequent basis?

447. Is there an on-going process in place to monitor Public Health Advisor project risks?

448. Are the key elements of a Public Health Advisor project Charter present?

449. Scope of work – What is the likelihood and extent of potential future changes to the Public Health Advisor project scope?

450. Are tasks tracked by hours?

451. Are the Public Health Advisor project plans updated on a frequent basis?

2.21 Activity Cost Estimates: Public Health Advisor

452. Was it performed on time?

453. Were sponsors and decision makers available when needed outside regularly scheduled meetings?

454. Can you delete activities or make them inactive?

455. What is included in indirect cost being allocated?

456. Measurable - are the targets measurable?

457. Performance bond should always provide what part of the contract value?

458. What defines a successful Public Health Advisor project?

459. Eac -estimate at completion, what is the total job expected to cost?

460. Are cost subtotals needed?

461. Who & what determines the need for contracted services?

462. What makes a good activity description?

463. What were things that you did very well and want to do the same again on the next Public Health Advisor project?

464. What happens if you cannot produce the documentation for the single audit?

465. Were decisions made in a timely manner?

466. What communication items need improvement?

467. What is the Public Health Advisor projects sustainability strategy that will ensure Public Health Advisor project results will endure or be sustained?

468. How and when do you enter into Public Health Advisor project Procurement Management?

469. Is costing method consistent with study goals?

470. What is a Public Health Advisor project Management Plan?

471. Were the tasks or work products prepared by the consultant useful?

2.22 Cost Estimating Worksheet: Public Health Advisor

472. Is it feasible to establish a control group arrangement?

473. What additional Public Health Advisor project(s) could be initiated as a result of this Public Health Advisor project?

474. Is the Public Health Advisor project responsive to community need?

475. What is the purpose of estimating?

476. Value pocket identification & quantification what are value pockets?

477. What can be included?

478. Will the Public Health Advisor project collaborate with the local community and leverage resources?

479. Ask: are others positioned to know, are others credible, and will others cooperate?

480. What will others want?

481. Can a trend be established from historical performance data on the selected measure and are the criteria for using trend analysis or forecasting methods met?

482. How will the results be shared and to whom?

483. Who is best positioned to know and assist in identifying corresponding factors?

484. What happens to any remaining funds not used?

485. Identify the timeframe necessary to monitor progress and collect data to determine how the selected measure has changed?

486. What is the estimated labor cost today based upon this information?

487. Does the Public Health Advisor project provide innovative ways for stakeholders to overcome obstacles or deliver better outcomes?

488. What costs are to be estimated?

2.23 Cost Baseline: Public Health Advisor

489. How do you manage cost?

490. What does a good WBS NOT look like?

491. Have the actual milestone completion dates been compared to the approved schedule?

492. What would the life cycle costs be?

493. Does a process exist for establishing a cost baseline to measure Public Health Advisor project performance?

494. Escalation criteria met?

495. Have all the product or service deliverables been accepted by the customer?

496. How will cost estimates be used?

497. Are you asking management for something as a result of this update?

498. Has the Public Health Advisor project documentation been archived or otherwise disposed as described in the Public Health Advisor project communication plan?

499. Does the suggested change request seem to represent a necessary enhancement to the product?

500. Is the requested change request a result of changes in other Public Health Advisor project(s)?

501. How difficult will it be to do specific tasks on the Public Health Advisor project?

502. Have all approved changes to the cost baseline been identified and impact on the Public Health Advisor project documented?

503. Has operations management formally accepted responsibility for operating and maintaining the product(s) or service(s) delivered by the Public Health Advisor project?

504. What is the most important thing to do next to make your Public Health Advisor project successful?

505. How likely is it to go wrong?

506. Have all approved changes to the schedule baseline been identified and impact on the Public Health Advisor project documented?

2.24 Quality Management Plan: Public Health Advisor

507. How are training records kept?

508. How is equipment calibrated?

509. How is staff trained?

510. Is the amount of effort justified by the anticipated value of forming a new process?

511. How does your organization determine the requirements and product/service features important to customers?

512. What data do you gather/use/compile?

513. Who is approving the QAPP?

514. How does your organization make it easy for customers to seek assistance or complain?

515. Is a component/condition present?

516. How are your organizations compensation and recognition approaches and the performance management system used to reinforce high performance?

517. How are deviations from procedures handled?

518. You know what your customers expectations are

regarding this process?

519. What are your organizations current levels and trends for the already stated measures related to employee wellbeing, satisfaction, and development?

520. Do trained quality assurance auditors conduct the audits as defined in the Quality Management Plan and scheduled by the Public Health Advisor project manager?

521. Does the program use modeling in the permitting or decision-making processes?

522. Who gets results of work?

523. What has the QM Collaboration done?

524. How does your organization design processes to ensure others meet customer and others requirements?

525. How do senior leaders review organizational performance?

526. Methodology followed?

2.25 Quality Metrics: Public Health Advisor

527. Is a risk containment plan in place?

528. Is there a set of procedures to capture, analyze and act on quality metrics?

529. What approved evidence based screening tools can be used?

530. Are interface issues coordinated?

531. Are quality metrics defined?

532. Are there any open risk issues?

533. Has risk analysis been adequately reviewed?

534. What is the timeline to meet your goal?

535. How do you calculate corresponding metrics?

536. Which data do others need in one place to target areas of improvement?

537. How do you measure?

538. How do you communicate results and findings to upper management?

539. Was the overall quality better or worse than previous products?

540. Was review conducted per standard protocols?

541. Is quality culture a competitive advantage?

542. Was material distributed on time?

543. What metrics do you measure?

544. Did evaluation start on time?

545. What happens if you get an abnormal result?

2.26 Process Improvement Plan: Public Health Advisor

546. Where do you focus?

547. The motive is determined by asking, Why do you want to achieve this goal?

548. Who should prepare the process improvement action plan?

549. Purpose of goal: the motive is determined by asking, why do you want to achieve this goal?

550. What is the test-cycle concept?

551. Have the frequency of collection and the points in the process where measurements will be made been determined?

552. Management commitment at all levels?

553. Does your process ensure quality?

554. What personnel are the coaches for your initiative?

555. Why do you want to achieve the goal?

556. Are you following the quality standards?

557. What personnel are the sponsors for that initiative?

558. What personnel are the change agents for your initiative?

559. What lessons have you learned so far?

560. Where do you want to be?

561. Everyone agrees on what process improvement is, right?

562. What actions are needed to address the problems and achieve the goals?

563. Are you making progress on the goals?

564. Has a process guide to collect the data been developed?

565. What makes people good SPI coaches?

2.27 Responsibility Assignment Matrix: Public Health Advisor

566. Does the Public Health Advisor project need to be analyzed further to uncover additional responsibilities?

567. The anticipated business volume?

568. Do work packages consist of discrete tasks which are adequately described?

569. Are estimates of costs at completion generated in a rational, consistent manner?

570. Are the actual costs used for variance analysis reconcilable with data from the accounting system?

571. The already stated responsible for the establishment of budgets and assignment of resources for overhead performance?

572. What are the known stakeholder requirements?

573. Are the requirements for all items of overhead established by rational, traceable processes?

574. Past experience – the person or the group worked at something similar in the past?

575. Authorization to proceed with all authorized work?

576. What expertise is not available in your department?

577. Wbs elements contractually specified for reporting of status (lowest level only)?

578. Identify and isolate causes of favorable and unfavorable cost and schedule variances?

579. Why cost benefit analysis?

580. Too many rs: with too many people labeled as doing the work, are there too many hands involved?

581. Too many is: do all the identified roles need to be routinely informed or only in exceptional circumstances?

582. Does the contractor use objective results, design reviews and tests to trace schedule performance?

583. Is work progressively subdivided into detailed work packages as requirements are defined?

2.28 Roles and Responsibilities: Public Health Advisor

584. Are your budgets supportive of a culture of quality data?

585. What specific behaviors did you observe?

586. Who is responsible for each task?

587. Who is responsible for implementation activities and where will the functions, roles and responsibilities be defined?

588. Key conclusions and recommendations: Are conclusions and recommendations relevant and acceptable?

589. Are the quality assurance functions and related roles and responsibilities clearly defined?

590. What expectations were met?

591. Are Public Health Advisor project team roles and responsibilities identified and documented?

592. Once the responsibilities are defined for the Public Health Advisor project, have the deliverables, roles and responsibilities been clearly communicated to every participant?

593. What should you do now to prepare for your career 5+ years from now?

594. How well did the Public Health Advisor project Team understand the expectations of specific roles and responsibilities?

595. Be specific; avoid generalities. Thank you and great work alone are insufficient. What exactly do you appreciate and why?

596. Was the expectation clearly communicated?

597. What expectations were NOT met?

598. What are your major roles and responsibilities in the area of performance measurement and assessment?

599. Concern: where are you limited or have no authority, where you can not influence?

600. What areas of supervision are challenging for you?

601. Attainable / achievable: the goal is attainable; can you actually accomplish the goal?

602. What areas would you highlight for changes or improvements?

2.29 Human Resource Management Plan: Public Health Advisor

603. Public Health Advisor project Objectives?

604. Who is evaluated?

605. Does the business case include how the Public Health Advisor project aligns with your organizations strategic goals & objectives?

606. Do all stakeholders know how to access this repository and where to find the Public Health Advisor project documentation?

607. Are Public Health Advisor project contact logs kept up to date?

608. Is the quality assurance team identified?

609. Are software metrics formally captured, analyzed and used as a basis for other Public Health Advisor project estimates?

610. Is the communication plan being followed?

611. Have the key elements of a coherent Public Health Advisor project management strategy been established?

612. Are risk oriented checklists used during risk identification?

613. Are the schedule estimates reasonable given the Public Health Advisor project?

614. Are change requests logged and managed?

615. Does the Public Health Advisor project have a Statement of Work?

616. Does the schedule include Public Health Advisor project management time and change request analysis time?

2.30 Communications Management Plan: Public Health Advisor

617. Is there an important stakeholder who is actively opposed and will not receive messages?

618. What is Public Health Advisor project communications management?

619. Why manage stakeholders?

620. Are the stakeholders getting the information others need, are others consulted, are concerns addressed?

621. How did the term stakeholder originate?

622. Can you think of other people who might have concerns or interests?

623. What data is going to be required?

624. Are stakeholders internal or external?

625. What to know?

626. Are others needed?

627. Do you feel a register helps?

628. Do you prepare stakeholder engagement plans?

629. Who to share with?

630. Who is the stakeholder?

631. How were corresponding initiatives successful?

632. How will the person responsible for executing the communication item be notified?

633. Who have you worked with in past, similar initiatives?

634. Where do team members get information?

2.31 Risk Management Plan: Public Health Advisor

635. Risk probability and impact: how will the probabilities and impacts of risk items be assessed?

636. Are you on schedule?

637. What are the chances the risk event will occur?

638. Litigation – what is the probability that lawsuits will cause problems or delays in the Public Health Advisor project?

639. Are tools for analysis and design available?

640. Financial risk: can your organization afford to undertake the Public Health Advisor project?

641. Why do you need to manage Public Health Advisor project Risk?

642. Risks should be identified during which phase of Public Health Advisor project management life cycle?

643. What will the damage be?

644. What other risks are created by choosing an avoidance strategy?

645. Is the number of people on the Public Health Advisor project team adequate to do the job?

646. Where are you confronted with risks during the business phases?

647. Are the metrics meaningful and useful?

648. People risk -are people with appropriate skills available to help complete the Public Health Advisor project?

649. Do you have a consistent repeatable process that is actually used?

650. Can it be changed quickly?

651. Does the Public Health Advisor project team have experience with the technology to be implemented?

652. How is risk monitoring performed?

653. Was an original risk assessment/risk management plan completed?

2.32 Risk Register: Public Health Advisor

654. What will be done?

655. Are your objectives at risk?

656. When would you develop a risk register?

657. What is the appropriate level of risk management for this Public Health Advisor project?

658. What action, if any, has been taken to respond to the risk?

659. How often will the Risk Management Plan and Risk Register be formally reviewed, and by whom?

660. Are implemented controls working as others should?

661. What are your key risks/show istoppers and what is being done to manage them?

662. Manageability – have mitigations to the risk been identified?

663. What may happen or not go according to plan?

664. Assume the risk event or situation happens, what would the impact be?

665. Cost/benefit – how much will the proposed

mitigations cost and how does this cost compare with the potential cost of the risk event/situation should it occur?

666. How is a Community Risk Register created?

667. Are there other alternative controls that could be implemented?

668. How are risks graded?

669. When will it happen?

670. Are there any gaps in the evidence?

671. When is it going to be done?

672. What should the audit role be in establishing a risk management process?

673. Risk categories: what are the main categories of risks that should be addressed on this Public Health Advisor project?

2.33 Probability and Impact Assessment: Public Health Advisor

674. What should be the level of coordination?

675. Your customers business requirements have suddenly shifted because of a new regulatory statute, what now?

676. Are the risk data complete?

677. Does the customer understand the software process?

678. Risk categorization -which of your categories has more risk than others?

679. What should be the external organizations responsibility vis-à-vis total stake in the Public Health Advisor project?

680. Will new information become available during the Public Health Advisor project?

681. How are the local factors going to affect the absorption?

682. What is the likelihood?

683. Are there alternative opinions/solutions/ processes you should explore?

684. Who should be responsible for the monitoring

and tracking of the indicators youhave identified?

685. My Public Health Advisor project leader has suddenly left your organization, what do you do?

686. How do risks change during the Public Health Advisor projects life cycle?

687. How much is the probability of a risk occurring?

688. Do the people have the right combinations of skills?

689. Who will be responsible for a slippage?

690. Is the technology to be built new to your organization?

691. Is a software Public Health Advisor project management tool available?

692. What are the uncertainties associated with the technology selected for the Public Health Advisor project?

693. Are the facilities, expertise, resources, and management know-how available to handle the situation?

2.34 Probability and Impact Matrix: Public Health Advisor

694. What should be done with non-critical risks?

695. Sensitivity analysis -which risks will have the most impact on the Public Health Advisor project?

696. Brain storm – mind maps, what if?

697. Which is the BEST thing to do?

698. Can you stabilize dynamic risk factors?

699. How do you analyze the risks in the different types of Public Health Advisor projects?

700. What should be done with risks on the watch list?

701. Does the software engineering team have the right mix of skills?

702. How solid are the price-volume Public Health Advisor projections?

703. How risk averse are you?

704. Is the Public Health Advisor project cutting across the entire organization?

705. Is the present organizational structure for handling the Public Health Advisor project sufficient?

706. What has the Public Health Advisor project manager forgotten to do?

707. Are people attending meetings and doing work?

708. During which risk management process is a determination to transfer a risk made?

709. What is the political situation at present?

710. How would you define a risk?

711. What do you expect?

2.35 Risk Data Sheet: Public Health Advisor

712. Has the most cost-effective solution been chosen?

713. What actions can be taken to eliminate or remove risk?

714. Do effective diagnostic tests exist?

715. How do you handle product safely?

716. If it happens, what are the consequences?

717. What was measured?

718. How reliable is the data source?

719. How can hazards be reduced?

720. What can you do?

721. Who has a vested interest in how you perform as your organization (our stakeholders)?

722. What can happen?

723. What are the main threats to your existence?

724. What are the main opportunities available to you that you should grab while you can?

725. How can it happen?

726. Whom do you serve (customers)?

727. What are you trying to achieve (Objectives)?

728. Are new hazards created?

729. What will be the consequences if it happens?

730. Type of risk identified?

731. Risk of what?

2.36 Procurement Management Plan: Public Health Advisor

732. How will multiple providers be managed?

733. Are post milestone Public Health Advisor project reviews (PMPR) conducted with your organization at least once a year?

734. How and when do you enter into Public Health Advisor project Procurement Management?

735. What types of contracts will be used?

736. Is there a procurement management plan in place?

737. Sensitivity analysis?

738. Is a payment system in place with proper reviews and approvals?

739. Are non-critical path items updated and agreed upon with the teams?

740. Is an industry recognized mechanized support tool(s) being used for Public Health Advisor project scheduling & tracking?

741. Has a sponsor been identified?

742. Have lessons learned been conducted after each Public Health Advisor project release?

743. Are adequate resources provided for the quality assurance function?

744. Have key stakeholders been identified?

745. Are schedule deliverables actually delivered?

746. Is there an onboarding process in place?

747. Is the steering committee active in Public Health Advisor project oversight?

748. Has the Public Health Advisor project manager been identified?

749. Is there an issues management plan in place?

2.37 Source Selection Criteria: Public Health Advisor

750. How much past performance information should be requested?

751. What should be considered when developing evaluation standards?

752. How should oral presentations be prepared for?

753. Do you want to have them collaborate at subfactor level?

754. How are clarifications and communications appropriately used?

755. Do proposed hours support content and schedule?

756. How can the methods of publicizing the buy be tailored to yield more effective price competition?

757. What should clarifications include?

758. Have all evaluators been trained?

759. What is the last item a Public Health Advisor project manager must do to finalize Public Health Advisor project close-out?

760. How do you facilitate evaluation against published criteria?

761. What is cost analysis and when should it be performed?

762. When is it appropriate to issue a DRFP?

763. Is this a cost contract?

764. What are the guiding principles for developing an evaluation report?

765. When must you conduct a debriefing?

766. If the costs are normalized, please account for how the normalization is conducted. Is a cost realism analysis used?

767. What procedures are followed when a contractor requires access to classified information or a significant quantity of special material/information?

768. How long will it take for the purchase cost to be the same as the lease cost?

769. Does your documentation identify why the team concurs or differs with reported performance from past performance report (CPARs, questionnaire responses, etc.)?

2.38 Stakeholder Management Plan: Public Health Advisor

770. Is the process working, and are people executing in compliance of the process?

771. Does the Public Health Advisor project have a Statement of Work?

772. Is stakeholder involvement adequate?

773. How will the equipment be verified?

774. Does all Public Health Advisor project documentation reside in a common repository for easy access?

775. Are trade-offs between accepting the risk and mitigating the risk identified?

776. What are the criteria for selecting suppliers of off the shelf products?

777. Have you eliminated all duplicative tasks or manual efforts, where appropriate?

778. Is it possible to track all classes of Public Health Advisor project work (e.g. scheduled, un-scheduled, defect repair, etc.)?

779. Has a provision been made to reassess Public Health Advisor project risks at various Public Health Advisor project stages?

780. Are metrics used to evaluate and manage Vendors?

781. What records are required (eg purchase orders, agreements)?

782. Have Public Health Advisor project management standards and procedures been established and documented?

783. What inspection and testing is to be performed?

784. Are stakeholders aware and supportive of the principles and practices of modern software estimation?

785. Is pert / critical path or equivalent methodology being used?

2.39 Change Management Plan: Public Health Advisor

786. What method and medium would you use to announce a message?

787. What is the negative impact of communicating too soon or too late?

788. How do you know the requirements you documented are the right ones?

789. What time commitment will this involve?

790. What new roles are needed?

791. What can you do to minimise misinterpretation and negative perceptions?

792. Who will fund the training?

793. Is there support for this application(s) and are the details available for distribution?

794. What risks may occur upfront?

795. When should a given message be communicated?

796. Have the business unit contacts been selected and notified?

797. What did the people around you say about it?

798. Change invariability confront many relationships especially the already stated that require a set of behaviours What roles with in your organization are affected and how?

799. Have the approved procedures and policies been published?

800. Why is the initiative is being undertaken - What are the business drivers?

801. What are the key change management success metrics?

802. Who might be able to help you the most?

803. Has a training need analysis been carried out?

3.0 Executing Process Group: Public Health Advisor

804. What are the critical steps involved with strategy mapping?

805. What are the critical steps involved in selecting measures and initiatives?

806. What are the main processes included in Public Health Advisor project quality management?

807. When is the appropriate time to bring the scorecard to Board meetings?

808. How will you avoid scope creep?

809. Are decisions made in a timely manner?

810. What is in place for ensuring adequate change control on Public Health Advisor projects that involve outside contracts?

811. What are crucial elements of successful Public Health Advisor project plan execution?

812. How could stakeholders negatively impact your Public Health Advisor project?

813. It under budget or over budget?

814. What are the main types of goods and services being outsourced?

815. How well did the chosen processes fit the needs of the Public Health Advisor project?

816. What type of people would you want on your team?

817. How well did the chosen processes produce the expected results?

818. What is involved in the solicitation process?

819. In what way has the program come up with innovative measures for problem-solving?

820. Do the partners have sufficient financial capacity to keep up the benefits produced by the programme?

821. How does Public Health Advisor project management relate to other disciplines?

3.1 Team Member Status Report: Public Health Advisor

822. Are the attitudes of staff regarding Public Health Advisor project work improving?

823. Do you have an Enterprise Public Health Advisor project Management Office (EPMO)?

824. Will the staff do training or is that done by a third party?

825. Is there evidence that staff is taking a more professional approach toward management of your organizations Public Health Advisor projects?

826. How it is to be done?

827. Does the product, good, or service already exist within your organization?

828. What specific interest groups do you have in place?

829. Does your organization have the means (staff, money, contract, etc.) to produce or to acquire the product, good, or service?

830. How much risk is involved?

831. The problem with Reward & Recognition Programs is that the truly deserving people all too often get left out. How can you make it practical?

832. How does this product, good, or service meet the needs of the Public Health Advisor project and your organization as a whole?

833. What is to be done?

834. Does every department have to have a Public Health Advisor project Manager on staff?

835. Are your organizations Public Health Advisor projects more successful over time?

836. How can you make it practical?

837. Why is it to be done?

838. Are the products of your organizations Public Health Advisor projects meeting customers objectives?

839. How will resource planning be done?

840. When a teams productivity and success depend on collaboration and the efficient flow of information, what generally fails them?

3.2 Change Request: Public Health Advisor

841. Will all change requests be unconditionally tracked through this process?

842. How are the measures for carrying out the change established?

843. What mechanism is used to appraise others of changes that are made?

844. Should a more thorough impact analysis be conducted?

845. Are you implementing itil processes?

846. Has a formal technical review been conducted to assess technical correctness?

847. How do team members communicate with each other?

848. What are the Impacts to your organization?

849. Who is responsible for the implementation and monitoring of all measures?

850. Since there are no change requests in your Public Health Advisor project at this point, what must you have before you begin?

851. Is it feasible to use requirements attributes as

predictors of reliability?

852. Describe how modifications, enhancements, defects and/or deficiencies shall be notified (e.g. Problem Reports, Change Requests etc) and managed. Detail warranty and/or maintenance periods?

853. How fast will change requests be approved?

854. When do you create a change request?

855. What is the relationship between requirements attributes and reliability?

856. Will there be a change request form in use?

857. How to get changes (code) out in a timely manner?

858. Which requirements attributes affect the risk to reliability the most?

859. Who needs to approve change requests?

860. How well do experienced software developers predict software change?

3.3 Change Log: Public Health Advisor

861. When was the request approved?

862. Will the Public Health Advisor project fail if the change request is not executed?

863. Does the suggested change request represent a desired enhancement to the products functionality?

864. Is the requested change request a result of changes in other Public Health Advisor project(s)?

865. Who initiated the change request?

866. Is the change request open, closed or pending?

867. Do the described changes impact on the integrity or security of the system?

868. When was the request submitted?

869. How does this change affect the timeline of the schedule?

870. Where do changes come from?

871. Is the submitted change a new change or a modification of a previously approved change?

872. How does this relate to the standards developed for specific business processes?

873. Is the change backward compatible without

limitations?

874. Is the change request within Public Health Advisor project scope?

875. How does this change affect scope?

876. Is this a mandatory replacement?

3.4 Decision Log: Public Health Advisor

877. It becomes critical to track and periodically revisit both operational effectiveness; Are you noticing all that you need to, and are you interpreting what you see effectively?

878. How does the use a Decision Support System influence the strategies/tactics or costs?

879. What alternatives/risks were considered?

880. What was the rationale for the decision?

881. Decision-making process; how will the team make decisions?

882. Is your opponent open to a non-traditional workflow, or will it likely challenge anything you do?

883. At what point in time does loss become unacceptable?

884. What is the line where eDiscovery ends and document review begins?

885. What is the average size of your matters in an applicable measurement?

886. Linked to original objective?

887. How effective is maintaining the log at

facilitating organizational learning?

888. What eDiscovery problem or issue did your organization set out to fix or make better?

889. Does anything need to be adjusted?

890. Adversarial environment. is your opponent open to a non-traditional workflow, or will it likely challenge anything you do?

891. How do you define success?

892. Is everything working as expected?

893. Meeting purpose; why does this team meet?

894. How consolidated and comprehensive a story can you tell by capturing currently available incident data in a central location and through a log of key decisions during an incident?

895. Who will be given a copy of this document and where will it be kept?

896. Behaviors; what are guidelines that the team has identified that will assist them with getting the most out of team meetings?

3.5 Quality Audit: Public Health Advisor

897. Are there appropriate indicators for monitoring the effectiveness and efficiency of processes?

898. How does your organization know that its systems for communicating with and among staff are appropriately effective and constructive?

899. What is your organizations greatest strength?

900. Are goals well supported with strategies, operational plans, manuals and training?

901. Are all records associated with the reconditioning of a device maintained for a minimum of two years after the sale or disposal of the last device within a lot of merchandise?

902. Are complaint files maintained?

903. What experience do staff have in the type of work that the audit entails?

904. How does your organization know that its advisory services are appropriately effective and constructive?

905. Are people allowed to contribute ideas?

906. How does your organization know that its relationships with the community at large are

appropriately effective and constructive?

907. How does your organization know that its research programs are appropriately effective and constructive?

908. Are the review comments incorporated?

909. How does the organization know that its system for maintaining and advancing the capabilities of its staff, particularly in relation to the Mission of the organization, is appropriately effective and constructive?

910. How does your organization know that the quality of its supervisors is appropriately effective and constructive?

911. Are all employees including salespersons made aware that they must report all complaints received from any source for inclusion in the complaint handling system?

912. Do prior clients have a positive opinion of your organization?

913. Do all staff have the necessary authority and resources to deliver what is expected of them?

914. How does your organization know that its management system is appropriately effective and constructive?

915. Are the intentions consistent with external obligations (such as applicable laws)?

916. Does the suppliers quality system have a written procedure for corrective action when a defect occurs?

3.6 Team Directory: Public Health Advisor

917. Why is the work necessary?

918. Who will report Public Health Advisor project status to all stakeholders?

919. What needs to be communicated?

920. What are you going to deliver or accomplish?

921. Process decisions: are contractors adequately prosecuting the work?

922. Does a Public Health Advisor project team directory list all resources assigned to the Public Health Advisor project?

923. Decisions: is the most suitable form of contract being used?

924. How does the team resolve conflicts and ensure tasks are completed?

925. How do unidentified risks impact the outcome of the Public Health Advisor project?

926. How will you accomplish and manage the objectives?

927. When does information need to be distributed?

928. Do purchase specifications and configurations match requirements?

929. Where will the product be used and/or delivered or built when appropriate?

930. Contract requirements complied with?

931. Process decisions: are there any statutory or regulatory issues relevant to the timely execution of work?

932. Who will be the stakeholders on your next Public Health Advisor project?

933. Who will talk to the customer?

934. Process decisions: are all start-up, turn over and close out requirements of the contract satisfied?

935. Have you decided when to celebrate the Public Health Advisor projects completion date?

3.7 Team Operating Agreement: Public Health Advisor

936. Did you delegate tasks such as taking meeting minutes, presenting a topic and soliciting input?

937. Do you upload presentation materials in advance and test the technology?

938. Do you ensure that all participants know how to use the required technology?

939. Did you recap the meeting purpose, time, and expectations?

940. How will group handle unplanned absences?

941. Are leadership responsibilities shared among team members (versus a single leader)?

942. To whom do you deliver your services?

943. Do you send out the agenda and meeting materials in advance?

944. What are the boundaries (organizational or geographic) within which you operate?

945. What is culture?

946. Do you ask participants to close laptops and place mobile devices on silent on the table while the meeting is in progress?

947. Do team members need to frequently communicate as a full group to make timely decisions?

948. How will you resolve conflict efficiently and respectfully?

949. Is compensation based on team and individual performance?

950. Resource allocation: how will individual team members account for time and expenses, and how will this be allocated in the team budget?

951. What are some potential sources of conflict among team members?

952. Did you draft the meeting agenda?

953. What administrative supports will be put in place to support the team and the teams supervisor?

954. Do you listen for voice tone and word choice to understand the meaning behind words?

955. Have you established procedures that team members can follow to work effectively together, such as a team operating agreement?

3.8 Team Performance Assessment: Public Health Advisor

956. If you have criticized someones work for method variance in your role as reviewer, what was the circumstance?

957. To what degree do the goals specify concrete team work products?

958. To what degree do team members understand one anothers roles and skills?

959. Can team performance be reliably measured in simulator and live exercises using the same assessment tool?

960. To what degree are the relative importance and priority of the goals clear to all team members?

961. To what degree do all members feel responsible for all agreed-upon measures?

962. To what degree does the teams approach to its work allow for modification and improvement over time?

963. To what degree can team members meet frequently enough to accomplish the teams ends?

964. Do you promptly inform members about major developments that may affect them?

965. Which situations call for a more extreme type of adaptiveness in which team members actually re-define roles?

966. To what degree does the teams purpose contain themes that are particularly meaningful and memorable?

967. Individual task proficiency and team process behavior: what is important for team functioning?

968. To what degree can the team ensure that all members are individually and jointly accountable for the teams purpose, goals, approach, and work-products?

969. To what degree are the goals realistic?

970. Can familiarity breed backup?

971. What are teams?

972. To what degree do members articulate the goals beyond the team membership?

973. To what degree are the goals ambitious?

974. To what degree does the teams work approach provide opportunity for members to engage in results-based evaluation?

975. Does more radicalness mean more perceived benefits?

3.9 Team Member Performance Assessment: Public Health Advisor

976. Does statute or regulation require the job responsibility?

977. How do you start collaborating?

978. How will they be formed?

979. To what degree are the teams goals and objectives clear, simple, and measurable?

980. What qualities does a successful Team leader possess?

981. How do you determine which data are the most important to use, analyze, or review?

982. To what extent are systems and applications (e.g., game engine, mobile device platform) utilized?

983. Who they are?

984. To what degree can all members engage in open and interactive considerations?

985. Who should attend?

986. Who is responsible?

987. What are the evaluation strategies (e.g., reaction, learning, behavior, results) used. What evaluation

results did you have?

988. New skills/knowledge gained this year?

989. What are best practices in use for the performance measurement system?

990. How do you know that all team members are learning?

991. What innovations (if any) are developed to realize goals?

992. What are acceptable governance changes?

993. What is the target group for instruction (e.g., individual and collective or small team instruction)?

3.10 Issue Log: Public Health Advisor

994. What does the stakeholder need from the team?

995. How often do you engage with stakeholders?

996. Who reported the issue?

997. How is this initiative related to other portfolios, programs, or Public Health Advisor projects?

998. What is the impact on the risks?

999. What steps can you take for positive relationships?

1000. Do you often overlook a key stakeholder or stakeholder group?

1001. What is the impact on the Business Case?

1002. Are there potential barriers between the team and the stakeholder?

1003. Do you feel more overwhelmed by stakeholders?

1004. Which team member will work with each stakeholder?

1005. What is the stakeholders political influence?

1006. What is a change?

1007. Who needs to know and how much?

1008. Is access to the Issue Log controlled?

1009. Are the stakeholders getting the information they need, are they consulted, are concerns addressed?

4.0 Monitoring and Controlling Process Group: Public Health Advisor

1010. What departments are involved in its daily operation?

1011. Who needs to be involved in the planning?

1012. What is the timeline for the Public Health Advisor project?

1013. Is there adequate validation on required fields?

1014. What resources (both financial and non-financial) are available/needed?

1015. Is the program making progress in helping to achieve the set results?

1016. Were escalated issues resolved promptly?

1017. How many more potential communications channels were introduced by the discovery of the new stakeholders?

1018. Have operating capacities been created and/or reinforced in partners?

1019. Is there sufficient funding available for this?

1020. Are the services being delivered?

1021. What business situation is being addressed?

1022. What is the expected monetary value of the Public Health Advisor project?

1023. How is agile program management done?

1024. What were things that you did very well and want to do the same again on the next Public Health Advisor project?

1025. Use: how will they use the information?

4.1 Project Performance Report: Public Health Advisor

1026. To what degree does the teams work approach provide opportunity for members to engage in fact-based problem solving?

1027. To what degree is the information network consistent with the structure of the formal organization?

1028. To what degree can team members vigorously define the teams purpose in considerations with others who are not part of the functioning team?

1029. To what degree does the task meet individual needs?

1030. To what degree do team members articulate the teams work approach?

1031. To what degree does the teams purpose constitute a broader, deeper aspiration than just accomplishing short-term goals?

1032. To what degree are the demands of the task compatible with and converge with the relationships of the informal organization?

1033. To what degree do team members agree with the goals, relative importance, and the ways in which achievement will be measured?

1034. To what degree can the team measure progress against specific goals?

1035. To what degree will each member have the opportunity to advance his or her professional skills in all three of the above categories while contributing to the accomplishment of the teams purpose and goals?

1036. To what degree does the funding match the requirement?

1037. To what degree do team members frequently explore the teams purpose and its implications?

1038. To what degree does the informal organization make use of individual resources and meet individual needs?

1039. To what degree does the team possess adequate membership to achieve its ends?

1040. What is the PRS?

1041. What degree are the relative importance and priority of the goals clear to all team members?

4.2 Variance Analysis: Public Health Advisor

1042. Are there changes in the overhead pool and/or organization structures?

1043. How do you verify authorization to proceed with all authorized work?

1044. Are all budgets assigned to control accounts?

1045. Can the relationship with problem customers be restructured so that there is a win-win situation?

1046. Who is generally responsible for monitoring and taking action on variances?

1047. How does your organization measure performance?

1048. How do you identify potential or actual overruns and underruns?

1049. What can be the cause of an increase in costs?

1050. What are the direct labor dollars and/or hours?

1051. Are your organizations and items of cost assigned to each pool identified?

1052. Are all elements of indirect expense identified to overhead cost budgets of Public Health Advisor projections?

1053. When, during the last four quarters, did a primary business event occur causing a fluctuation?

1054. Are the bases and rates for allocating costs from each indirect pool consistently applied?

1055. Other relevant issues of Variance Analysis -selling price or gross margin?

1056. Is budgeted cost for work performed calculated in a manner consistent with the way work is planned?

1057. What are the actual costs to date?

1058. What should management do?

4.3 Earned Value Status: Public Health Advisor

1059. Verification is a process of ensuring that the developed system satisfies the stakeholders agreements and specifications; Are you building the product right? What do you verify?

1060. Where is evidence-based earned value in your organization reported?

1061. How much is it going to cost by the finish?

1062. Validation is a process of ensuring that the developed system will actually achieve the stakeholders desired outcomes; Are you building the right product? What do you validate?

1063. Where are your problem areas?

1064. When is it going to finish?

1065. Are you hitting your Public Health Advisor projects targets?

1066. How does this compare with other Public Health Advisor projects?

1067. Earned value can be used in almost any Public Health Advisor project situation and in almost any Public Health Advisor project environment. it may be used on large Public Health Advisor projects, medium sized Public Health Advisor projects, tiny Public

Health Advisor projects (in cut-down form), complex and simple Public Health Advisor projects and in any market sector. some people, of course, know all about earned value, they have used it for years - but perhaps not as effectively as they could have?

1068. What is the unit of forecast value?

1069. If earned value management (EVM) is so good in determining the true status of a Public Health Advisor project and Public Health Advisor project its completion, why is it that hardly any one uses it in information systems related Public Health Advisor projects?

4.4 Risk Audit: Public Health Advisor

1070. Is the auditor truly independent?

1071. What are the outcomes you are looking for?

1072. What does internal control mean in the context of the audit process?

1073. Estimated size of product in number of programs, files, transactions?

1074. What are the benefits of a Enterprise wide approach to Risk Management?

1075. Do you have financial policies and procedures in place to guide officers of your organization/treasurer/ general members?

1076. If applicable; does the software interface with new or unproven hardware or unproven vendor products?

1077. Are end-users enthusiastically committed to the Public Health Advisor project and the system/product to be built?

1078. Does your organization have a register of insurance policies detailing all current insurance policies?

1079. Do you have written and signed agreements/ contracts in place for each paid staff member?

1080. Is your organization an exempt employer for payroll tax purposes?

1081. Does your board meet regularly and document all decisions and actions?

1082. Are formal technical reviews part of this process?

1083. When your organization is entering into a major contract, does it seek legal advice?

1084. Whence the business risk audit?

1085. Does the Public Health Advisor project team have experience with the technology to be implemented?

1086. What are the Internal Controls ?

1087. Are team members trained in the use of the tools?

4.5 Contractor Status Report: Public Health Advisor

1088. Are there contractual transfer concerns?

1089. Describe how often regular updates are made to the proposed solution. Are corresponding regular updates included in the standard maintenance plan?

1090. What was the actual budget or estimated cost for your organizations services?

1091. What was the budget or estimated cost for your organizations services?

1092. What was the final actual cost?

1093. How long have you been using the services?

1094. Who can list a Public Health Advisor project as organization experience, your organization or a previous employee of your organization?

1095. What was the overall budget or estimated cost?

1096. How is risk transferred?

1097. What are the minimum and optimal bandwidth requirements for the proposed soluiton?

1098. If applicable; describe your standard schedule for new software version releases. Are new software version releases included in the standard maintenance plan?

1099. What is the average response time for answering a support call?

1100. What process manages the contracts?

4.6 Formal Acceptance: Public Health Advisor

1101. What was done right?

1102. Who supplies data?

1103. Do you buy-in installation services?

1104. Was the Public Health Advisor project work done on time, within budget, and according to specification?

1105. What features, practices, and processes proved to be strengths or weaknesses?

1106. What lessons were learned about your Public Health Advisor project management methodology?

1107. Did the Public Health Advisor project manager and team act in a professional and ethical manner?

1108. Was business value realized?

1109. Was the client satisfied with the Public Health Advisor project results?

1110. Does it do what Public Health Advisor project team said it would?

1111. What can you do better next time?

1112. How does your team plan to obtain formal

acceptance on your Public Health Advisor project?

1113. Have all comments been addressed?

1114. Did the Public Health Advisor project achieve its MOV?

1115. Was the sponsor/customer satisfied?

1116. General estimate of the costs and times to complete the Public Health Advisor project?

1117. What are the requirements against which to test, Who will execute?

1118. What function(s) does it fill or meet?

1119. Does it do what client said it would?

1120. Was the Public Health Advisor project managed well?

5.0 Closing Process Group: Public Health Advisor

1121. What will you do?

1122. What can you do better next time, and what specific actions can you take to improve?

1123. How dependent is the Public Health Advisor project on other Public Health Advisor projects or work efforts?

1124. Did the Public Health Advisor project team have enough people to execute the Public Health Advisor project plan?

1125. What was learned?

1126. Did the Public Health Advisor project management methodology work?

1127. What areas were overlooked on this Public Health Advisor project?

1128. Based on your Public Health Advisor project communication management plan, what worked well?

1129. What is an Encumbrance?

1130. What is the amount of funding and what Public Health Advisor project phases are funded?

1131. Does the close educate others to improve performance?

1132. What level of risk does the proposed budget represent to the Public Health Advisor project?

1133. Was the user/client satisfied with the end product?

1134. What is the Public Health Advisor project name and date of completion?

5.1 Procurement Audit: Public Health Advisor

1135. In case of decisions not to conclude a procurement or award a contract, were tenderers informed in writing and on a timely basis of the already stated decisions and grounds?

1136. Are existing suppliers that have a special right to be consulted being contacted?

1137. How do you avoid delays at any stage/ stages of the procurement process?

1138. Who is verifying the performance of the contract and approving payments?

1139. Have the funding arrangements been agreed where payments take place over several financial periods?

1140. Do established procedures ensure that computer programs will not pay the same group of invoices twice?

1141. Is your organization aware and informed about international procurement standards and good practice?

1142. Are criteria and sub-criteria set suitable to identify the tender that offers best value for money?

1143. Do staff involved in the various stages of the

process have the appropriate skills and training to perform duties effectively?

1144. Is each copy of the purchase order necessary?

1145. In a competitive dialogue, were solutions proposed or confidential information given by a candidate not revealed to others without his/her express agreement?

1146. Must the receipt of goods be approved prior to payment?

1147. Does an appropriately qualified official check the quality of performance against the contract terms?

1148. Does the procurement function/unit understand costumer needs, supply markets and suppliers?

1149. If the expert was allowed to submit a tender, was all the relevant information the expert had gained from his earlier involvement made available to the other bidders?

1150. Is there a form specified for bids?

1151. Has your organization procedures in place to monitor the input of experts employed to assist the procurement function?

1152. Are incentives to deliver on time and in quantity properly specified?

1153. Does the strategy include a policy for

identifying and training suitable procurement staff?

1154. Does procurement staff have recognized professional procurement qualifications or sufficient training?

5.2 Contract Close-Out: Public Health Advisor

1155. How/when used ?

1156. Have all acceptance criteria been met prior to final payment to contractors?

1157. Parties: Authorized?

1158. Change in knowledge?

1159. What happens to the recipient of services?

1160. Change in attitude or behavior?

1161. Have all contract records been included in the Public Health Advisor project archives?

1162. Was the contract complete without requiring numerous changes and revisions?

1163. Have all contracts been closed?

1164. How does it work?

1165. Are the signers the authorized officials?

1166. Has each contract been audited to verify acceptance and delivery?

1167. Parties: who is involved?

1168. Why Outsource?

1169. Was the contract type appropriate?

1170. What is capture management?

1171. Was the contract sufficiently clear so as not to result in numerous disputes and misunderstandings?

1172. How is the contracting office notified of the automatic contract close-out?

1173. Change in circumstances?

1174. Have all contracts been completed?

5.3 Project or Phase Close-Out: Public Health Advisor

1175. What process was planned for managing issues/risks?

1176. Who controlled the resources for the Public Health Advisor project?

1177. What was expected from each stakeholder?

1178. What advantages do the an individual interview have over a group meeting, and vice-versa?

1179. What is the information level of detail required for each stakeholder?

1180. What are they?

1181. Can the lesson learned be replicated?

1182. What is a Risk?

1183. What information is each stakeholder group interested in?

1184. Were the outcomes different from the already stated planned?

1185. What were the desired outcomes?

1186. Who is responsible for award close-out?

1187. What were the actual outcomes?

1188. What is a Risk Management Process?

1189. What could have been improved?

1190. What is this stakeholder expecting?

1191. Were messages directly related to the release strategy or phases of the Public Health Advisor project?

1192. What are the informational communication needs for each stakeholder?

1193. Were risks identified and mitigated?

1194. What went well?

5.4 Lessons Learned: Public Health Advisor

1195. How well did the scope of the Public Health Advisor project match what was defined in the Public Health Advisor project Proposal?

1196. How effective was the support you received during implementation of the product/service?

1197. How efficient and effective were Public Health Advisor project team meetings?

1198. How well did the Public Health Advisor project Manager respond to questions or comments related to the Public Health Advisor project?

1199. What was the methodology behind successful learning experiences, and how might they be applied to the broader challenge of your organizations knowledge management?

1200. How well does the product or service the Public Health Advisor project produced meet the defined Public Health Advisor project requirements?

1201. Was the necessary hardware, software, accommodation etc available?

1202. What things surprised you on the Public Health Advisor project that were not in the plan?

1203. Was Public Health Advisor project performance

validated or challenged?

1204. Which estimation issues did you personally have and what was the impact?

1205. How was the quality of products/processes assured?

1206. What was the geopolitical history during the origin of your organization and at the time of task input?

1207. What things mattered the most on this Public Health Advisor project?

1208. How effective were the communications materials in providing and orienting team members about the details of the Public Health Advisor project?

1209. How effective was the architecture/system design process?

1210. How did the estimated Public Health Advisor project Budget compare with the total actual expenditures?

1211. How well defined were the acceptance criteria for Public Health Advisor project deliverables?

1212. How effective were Best Practices & Lessons Learned from prior Public Health Advisor projects utilized in this Public Health Advisor project?

1213. Was the Public Health Advisor project significantly delayed/hampered by outside dependencies (outside to the Public Health Advisor project, that is)?

1214. How clear were you on your role in the Public Health Advisor project?

Index

company	7, 106, 108, 123, 128
compare	209, 253, 271
compared	36, 164, 190
comparison	12
compatible	125, 230, 249
compelling	31
compete	113, 128
competing	42
Competitor	142
compile	192
compiling	122
complain	192
complaint	234-235
complaints	235
complete	1, 9, 12, 26, 50, 167-168, 172, 176, 179-180, 207, 210, 260, 266
completed	13, 25, 33-34, 172, 184, 207, 237, 267
completing	161, 172
completion	30, 32, 172, 186, 190, 198, 238, 254, 262
complex	7, 50, 128, 134, 146, 254
complexity	39, 44-45
compliance	36, 39, 93, 97, 100-101, 110, 114, 133-134, 139, 158, 220
compliancy	119
compliant	105, 109, 114, 122, 125, 127, 133
complied	238
comply	87, 112-113, 125
complying	126
component	192
components	40, 44, 149, 162
comprise	144
compute	13
computer	263
concept	103, 196
concepts	159
conceptual	179
Concern	201
concerned	24
Concerning	19
concerns	22, 24, 109, 112-113, 123, 204, 246, 257
concise	151
conclude	263
concrete	122, 241

295

CPSIA information can be obtained
at www.ICGtesting.com
Printed in the USA
BVHW080803220419
546159BV00025B/1680/P